CONSTRUCTION SCHEDULING SIMPLIFIED

CONSTRUCTION SCHEDULING SIMPLIFIED

Anthony L. Iannone

Andrew M. Civitello, Jr.

Prentice-Hall, Inc.
Englewood Cliffs, NJ

Prentice-Hall International, Inc., *London*
Prentice-Hall of Australia, Pty. Ltd., *Sydney*
Prentice-Hall of Canada, Inc., *Toronto*
Prentice-Hall of India Private Ltd., *New Delhi*
Prentice-Hall of Japan, Inc., *Tokyo*
Prentice-Hall of Southeast Asia Pte. Ltd., *Singapore*
Whitehall Books, Ltd., Wellington, *New Zealand*
Editora Prentice-Hall do Brasil Ltda., *Rio de Janeiro*
Prentice-Hall Hispanoamericana, S.A., *Mexico*

© 1985 *by*

PRENTICE-HALL, INC.
Englewood Cliffs, N.J.

All rights reserved. No part of this
book may be reproduced in any form or
by any means, without permission in
writing from the publisher.

This publication is designed to provide information, facts, opinions, and ideas in regard to the subject matter covered. It is sold with the understanding that by this product neither the publisher nor the authors are engaged in rendering legal, accounting, or other professional service. If legal advice or other expert assistance is required, the services of a competent professional person should be sought.

10 9 8 7 6 5 4 3 2

Library of Congress Cataloging in Publication Data

Iannone, Anthony L.
  Construction scheduling simplified.

  Includes index.
    1. Construction industry—Management. 2. Scheduling
(Management) I. Civitello, Andrew M.,
II. Title.
HD9715.A2I248 1985   624′.068′5   84-26495

ISBN 0-13-168923-1

Printed in the United States of America

About the Authors

Anthony L. Iannone, Ph.D., Management Program Planning Specialist, invented the Management Operation System Technique (MOST), Line of Balance PUT/TAKE, and other useful scheduling techniques in 1962. The awards for his work in all phases of program and production planning, scheduling, and control have gained for him the leading position in his field.

During the last twenty years, he has taught PERT, CPM, MOST, LOB, Configuration Management/Control, and Program Management to many in business, industry, government, and at numerous universities. He has had six books and many articles published on his works, is a member of at least five speakers' lists locally and nationally, and has been a member of the Government/Industrial Committee for the Unification of PERT, PERT/COST and Scheduling.

Mr. Iannone studied mechanical engineering at the University of Connecticut, and science at the University of Bridgeport. He received his Bachelor of Science Degree from Century University of Management Science (Quantitative), and his Ph.D. in Business Administration with a concentration in Schedule Management from the Accredited University of California.

Andrew M. Civitello, Jr. has managed and controlled construction projects of every size and type since 1976. His clients include local and federal government agencies and departments, municipalities, banks, service organizations, and private developers. His contributions are the direct result of the consistently successful use and development of the MOST technique by a professional general contractor.

Mr. Civitello is also an independent scheduling and construction management consultant to contractors, subcontractors, and lawyers. He is an arbitrator for the American Arbitration Association, university instructor to senior engineers for project planning and scheduling, and is the author of the Construction Operations Manual of Policies and Procedures (published in 1982 by Prentice-Hall, Inc). He has led and participated in seminars presenting various topics related to the construction field.

Mr. Civitello studied civil engineering and received his Bachelor of Science Degree in Business Administration from Syracuse University.

Introduction

How can I streamline operations for maximum efficiency, economy, flexibility, and profits?"

This question haunts the minds of today's executives, managers, and owners in every industry from construction to zippers. As the operation grows larger and more complex, as the team gets bigger, as the tempo speeds up, executives begin to lose control because of:
* Undigested masses of data and reports
* Inability to alter plans because of unforeseen problems
* Weakness of "traditional" management methods
* Lack of timely "danger signals" to warn of slipping schedules and rising costs

It is impossible for the executive, unaided, to wade through all needed data, evaluate all potential problems and solutions, make a business plan, supervise its execution, and alter it when needed. You need help.

<u>Construction Scheduling Simplified</u> is the help you need. This book presents MOST (Management Operation System Technique) - a uniform, easy to use, tested, and <u>proven</u> technique for sustaining profitable operations and growth through inexpensive and effective planning and control.

The construction schedule is the fundamental tool that enables all levels of management to plan, operate, and control in a professional, coordinated manner. The MOST Simplified Construction Scheduling System, like a ballistic missile autopilot, is goal-seeking by design. When programmed with specific data, an autopilot seeks a target unerringly through the use of feedback. If not programmed, or if programmed with vague, incorrect, or incomplete data, the device will wander aimlessly until its propulsion system fails, or until it self-destructs.

Likewise, the MOST Simplified Construction Scheduling System is the action plan that <u>programs</u> management toward the attainment of the ultimate goal of higher profits through successful project completion. The feedback mechanism of fast, easy, and inexpensive periodic revisions continually corrects the plan relative to its original objectives to keep on target and finish each project under control. If a project is begun without a schedule or with a schedule that has been inadequately prepared, is too complicated for everyone to understand, or is otherwise inappropriate, management direction will be unclear. Project people will then jump from fire to fire in an uncoordinated, wasteful process - until the management propulsion system, like the autopilot, fails, or until it self destructs.

In short, if you fail to plan, you plan to fail by default. The consequences: inefficiency, lawsuits, bad reputations, and inevitable erosion of profits.

In addition to good planning, cost-effective monitoring and controlling of construction projects are crucial for sustained growth and maximum profits. With the increase in the use of computers, ever increasing specification requirements, and the barrage of government regulation, it has become absolutely necessary to report field information quickly and accurately, while reducing reporting time. Dramatic increases in the cost of doing business dictate that you must streamline operations for maximum efficiency and eliminate waste if you are to control overhead and stay in business. Finally, increases in the incidence of arbitration and court litigation mean that if you are to get and stay on top, all of your records must be timely, accurate, complete, properly documented and easily correlated.

The MOST system in Construction Scheduling Simplified not only __addresses__ these needs, it also __fulfills__ them.

Why MOST is a must

The Management Operation System Technique (MOST) is the latest fast-tracked project management system that by:
* Saving you time,
* Simplifying your work,
* Saving you money, and
* Building your profits,

will allow you to break away from your competition and move ahead fast.

MOST is the construction scheduling technique and project control method which has as its fundamental strength the most significant improvements to the construction control process since CPM - it's fast, easy, and inexpensive.

In recent years, Critical Path Method (CPM) was developed for the construction and industrial businesses. Since CPM's inception, Mr. Iannone has taught the CPM system to many people in the United States and abroad. But by 1963, he realized that a more direct and easy to use scheduling technique was badly needed to provide quicker visibility and to be more economical than CPM. In construction projects where CPM is used, a computer is required. With MOST, a computer is not necessary, and fewer people and resources are needed for its adoption.

MOST has replaced CPM in construction circles here and abroad with great success. It has been used in constructing many complex construction projects of every size and type - from $30,000 additions, to $190 million high rises, to the prestigious U.S.S. Nautilus Memorial. (In the latter case, the U.S. Navy promptly dropped a 6-page boilerplate requiring CPM on the project in favor of MOST. The savings realized in the scheduling budget topped $20,000.) For those people who may still prefer to use CPM to plan a project, they can easily convert their CPM to MOST for monitoring and reporting actual status on a timely basis. This combination makes a unique package system for management planning and scheduling control. This concept will provide:
* System package control,
* Better economy that CPM alone,
* Better project budgeting,
* Continuous finger-tip controls for the project manager and field superintendent.

The cost of the use of the MOST system is a fraction of the cost of CPM. Once a MOST schedule is drawn and approved, each updating cycle will take one hour or less, regardless of project size.

MOST...

...Is Visual
Just as you can get the visual impact and obvious trends and outlooks by reviewing graphs rather than by reading tables of data, with MOST you can actually see the status of a project without having to sift through all the detail. You can tell how the job is going by looking at the schedule, without reading through all the detail.

...Is Easy to Learn
The step by step instruction, simplified rules of thumb, clear illustrations, charts, and diagrams make learning and understanding rapid and complete. No drafting ability is required - only basic arithmetic.

...Is Inexpensive
The only investment that you'll need to make beyond this book is in a roll of drafting vellum, a pencil, and a ruler. This modest investment will allow you to schedule projects of any size and complexity. This immediately saves you thousands of dollars when compared to any other scheduling technique requiring a computer and/or personnel with specialized training.

...Is Fast
Updating takes, at most, one hour per update - regardless of project size - to keep all records complete and accurate. This makes it easy for your people to be on time with their assignments. Its early warning system draws immediate attention to critical problems in time for appropriate management action before the project is impacted.

...Never Needs to Be Redrawn
No company resources ever need to be expended on re-generating a "new" schedule at each update. Again, the emphasis is on keeping costs down.

...Always Relates Actual Performance to the Original Plan
—not just back to the last revision. MOST keeps overall project performance in perspective; if a problem is brewing, MOST warns you in good time to allow you to take corrective action before things get out of control.

WHY MOST IS A MUST

...Is Easy to Present:
The fundamental logic of MOST and its graphic, visual format make it exceptionally easy to present to non-construction personnel such as arbitrators, judges and owners to be absolutely certain that your explanations, arguments, and defenses are well received and clearly understood. This has traditionally been the most significant disadvantage of CPM (Critical Path Method) and other complicated computer scheduling techniques.

...Facilitates Orderly, Speedy, and Complete Job Meetings.
MOST provides a convenient focal point from which to conduct brief, professional job meetings. It enables you to nail down commitments that would otherwise be too easily shifted onto the back burner. It eliminates procrastination and confirms the prompt resolution of "field conditions," "clarifications," "changes," and so on. You'll avoid inadvertently overlooking important items that require open discussion. You'll control the proceedings and the timing of discussions at your meetings - not the architect.

...Helps Prevent Serious Disputes
The use of MOST will prevent acrimonious disputes from arising over backcharges, delay claims, interference charges, and the like. This is because it demonstrates the direct results of any party's actions - or inactions - on the construction sequence. The architect, the engineers, and the owner are placed on the schedule just as you are, making it impossible to pass the buck.

...Increases Cooperation from Subcontractors.
Because they know MOST is watching them, subcontractors make a special effort to perform their work the way you want - within the alotted time frame.

...Generates Internal Schedules
MOST enables your people to quickly coordinate material/equipment purchases, the timing of subcontract negotiations, material delivery lead times, and shop drawing preparation and submission. It eliminates the guesswork of these and other internal company activities.

...Will Improve Your Reputation.
MOST demontrates to clients, prospective clients, architects, owners, and your bonding company your ability to plan and direct your operation effectively and professionally. A track record of projects completed under control will go a long way in convincing your surety that the information you give them is based on record and not to be discounted.

...Will Increase Your Profits

By using MOST to exhibit greater control, improve your efficiency, and eliminate unnecessary overhead, you'll complete your projects on time or ahead of schedule. You'll cut out unnecessary office and field expenses, avoid damages due to delay, compliment your reputation as a competent, capable professional, and produce satisfied customers. Depending on the size of your company and the size of the individual project under consideration, a single day saved on a single project's completion by using MOST will mean immediate savings of hundreds to thousands of dollars in office overhead alone.

How to Use This Book

CONSTRUCTION SCHEDULING SIMPLIFIED will show you:

* How to make the owner and the architect as accountable to the construction progress as you are. (Chapter 1)

* How to easily construct and monitor a clear action plan for each construction project that will effectively guide all activities toward the profit objective. (Chapter 1)

* How to clearly show total change order impact on sequence and timing of planned work to put you in the best position for change order negotiation, claims, time extensions, and delays. (Chapter 2)

* How to simply and completely document and quantify specific responsibility for delays by subcontractors, the owner, and the design professionals. (Chapters 2, 3, 4)

* How to flag out foreseeable problems to allow you to implement corrective action in time to save your job's profit. (Chapter 2)

* How to substantiate backcharges to subcontractors to end arguments before they begin. (Chapter 3)

* How to construct "Get-Well" plans to correct behind-schedule projects to finish on time - thereby saving your profits and your reputation. (Chapter 2)

* How to update the entire schedule in one hour or less - regardless of project size. (Chapter 1)

* How to quickly and simply incorporate all the elements legally required to insure that your schedules will always be presentable evidence in court or in arbitration. (Chapter 3)

* How to plan and manage manpower for maximum production efficiency. (Chapter 5)

* How to consolidate all projects into a simple, easy to read master production schedule that will enable management to quickly determine committed and available production capacity for short and long term production and financial planning. (Chapter 8)

* How to easily generate accurate cash-flow projections for use in preparation of cash budgets and investment planning. This information will enable financial management to anticipate the size and timing of receivables and payables to maximize investment opportunities while maintaining good credit standing. (Chapter 8)

* How to develop leadership abilities in yourself and in your subordinates to control every business situation with confidence and effective delegation. (Chapter 9)

* How to produce your "Countdown Schedules" to cleanly tie together all loose ends at the project's final phases, in order to avoid lingering punch-lists, and get your final payment in a reasonable amount of time. (Chapter 2)

The power of MOST lies in its simplicity. Its basic building block nature makes MOST valuable for all levels of management - from the most basic production considerations to strategic planning.

Because it's easy to use, it will be used.

Construction Scheduling Simplified is a step-by-step instructional manual designed to take you through the logical progression in the development, use, and presentation of MOST. From that point, the book progresses to more advanced topics and applications, and on to uses that permeate all other areas of the contracting business. The result is a complete presentation of the full power of MOST that develops from and lies in its simplicity and visibility.

Read through the book completely in order as arranged. This will keep the instruction in logical sequence to make your mastery of the material rapid and complete. After that, reread individual sections as appropriate, using the Table of Contents as a menu from which to select topics and instruction relative to your interests and needs as they occur. Refer back to the book when preparing each new schedule, but also reread occasionally to review uses of the technique that you or your company may not have been ready for when you first decided to implement MOST. Finally, be sure that your planning, site, and project management people all have a copy of Construction Scheduling Simplified at their disposal, not only to allow for their convenient

HOW TO USE THIS BOOK

research in the use of the MOST system, but to allow all at any level of site and home office management to continue their personal development as construction professionals.

Acknowledgments

The authors make grateful acknowledgment to the R. A. Civitello Company, in Woodbridge, Connecticut, for its generous release of some of the illustrations used. Also, we wish to express appreciation to Michele Masse Iannone, Gail Q. Civitello, and Linda Iannone for typing and editing the manuscript. Finally, to the many construction companies that have encouraged us to write this book, especially for their interpretation, adaptability, and use for successful scheduling.

IMPORTANT COPYRIGHT NOTICE:

Permission to use the full size forms, exhibits, and word-for-word letters is granted by the authors and publisher ONLY to purchasers of Construction Scheduling Simplified.

Illustrations

			Page
Figure	1-1	MOST Construction Techniques	30
Figure	1-2	MOST Construction Techniques	30
Figure	1-3	MOST Construction Techniques	30
Figure	1-4	MOST Construction Techniques	30
Figure	1-5	MOST Construction Techniques	30
Figure	1-6	MOST Construction Techniques	30
Figure	1-7	CPM vs MOST	32
Figure	1-8	MOST: Small One-Story Building	33
Figure	1-9	Percentage Completion	36
Figure	1-10	Percentage Completion	36
Figure	1-11	Percentage Completion	36
Figure	1-12	MOST Updating of Dog House	39
Figure	1-13	MOST Update of Industrial Project	40
Figure	1-14	Rescheduling Without Redrawing	41
Figure	1-15	Rescheduling Without Redrawing	43
Figure	1-15.A	Progress Update	44
Figure	1-16	Trend Analysis	45
Figure	1-17	Schedule Analysis and Evaluation Report Form	47
Figure	1-18	Variance Report	49
Figure	2-1	Typical Job Listing	56
Figure	2-2	Continue Job Listing	57
Figure	2-3	Continue Job Listing	57
Figure	2-4	High Riser Apartment	59
Figure	2-5	Contingencies or Down Time	61
Figure	2-6	High Riser Apartment - Update	62
Figure	2-7	Get-Well Plan	64
Figure	2-8	Complete MOST from Figure 1-8	66
Figure	2-9	Mini-MOST (Mechanical Subcontractor)	68
Figure	2-10	Sample Superintendent Bar Chart	70
Figure	2-11	Change Order Schedule	71
Figure	2-12	Notification of Change Order	75
Figure	2-13	Change Order Lead Times	76
Exhibit	1	Letter Requesting Change Order Proposal	79
Figure	2-14	Multiproject Schedule	82
Figure	2-15	Updated Multiproject Schedule	83
Figure	2-16	Countdown Schedule	85
Figure	3-1	Actual Work Performed	89
Figure	3-2	Change Order Effect	90
Figure	3-3	Slippages	91
Figure	3-4	Total Schedule Impact	91
Figure	3-4.A	Planned vs Actual Work	92
Figure	3-4.B	Planned vs Actual Work	93
Exhibit	2	Letter to Subcontractors and Suppliers Regarding Baseline Schedule Acknowledgment	100
Exhibit	3	Letter to Subcontractors and Suppliers Regarding Baseline Schedule Release	102

			Page
Exhibit	4	MOST Schedule Analysis/Evaluation Report	105
Figure	5-1	Manpower Loading	113
Figure	5-2	Manpower Leveling	114
Figure	6-1	MOST/COST	118
Figure	6-2	Posting Commitment	119
Figure	6-3	MOST/COST Tabulation	120
Figure	8-1	MOST for Financial Planning	128
Figure	8-1.A	Material Estimates	129
Figure	8-1.B	Material Estimates (Continued)	129
Figure	8-2.A	Labor Cost	131
Figure	8-2.B	Cost Assignment	131
Figure	8-3.A	Material Assignment	133
Figure	8-3.B	Detailed Cost Assignments	133
Figure	8-4.A	Total Cost	136
Figure	8-4.B	Projected Receivable Tabulation	136
Figure	8-5.A	Individual Cost	138
Figure	8-5.B	Cumulative Cost	138
Figure	8-6	Actual vs Projected Receivables	141
Figure	8-7	Receivable Status Tabulation	144
Figure	8-8	Complete Receivable Status Tabulation	145
Figure	8-9	Complete Receivable Status Tabulation (Optional Format)	146
Figure	8-10	Change Order Cost	149
Figure	8-11.A	Problem Area Curve	151
Figure	8-11.B	Projected vs Actual Receivables	152
Figure	8-11.C	Projected vs Actual Receivables	154
Figure	8-12	The Maxi-MOST Integration	157
Figure	9-1	The Major Attributes of Leadership	170
Figure	9-2	The Ten Major Causes of Failure in Leadership	171
Figure	10-1	Summary Plan from Figure 2-8	174

Appendix
Figure	A-1	Network of Paths	188
Figure	A-2	Critical Path	189
Figure	A-3	Network of T_E	190
Figure	A-4	Network Completion	191
Figure	A-5	CPM Total Calculations	192
Figure	A-6	CPM: Dog House Plan	194
Figure	A-7	CPM: Small One-Story Building	196

Table of Contents

INTRODUCTION.. 7
   Why MOST is a must.. 9
HOW TO USE THIS BOOK... 13
ACKNOWLEDGMENTS.. 17
HELP... 23

ONE

SIMPLIFIED PLANNING, SCHEDULING, AND CONTROL

1 Planning for Profit: The Management Operation System Technique................................ 27

    The MOST simplified scheduling technique......... 28
    Using MOST for construction...................... 29
    MOST vs CPM for better understanding............. 31
    The MOST EASY (ONE HOUR) UPDATE method........... 34
    Percentage of completion......................... 35
    Reschedule without redrawing with MOST........... 40
    Schedule analysis and evaluation................. 44

TWO

CONSTRUCTION SCHEDULING MADE EASY

2 The MOST Action Program for Project Control......... 53

    Preparation of the BASELINE SCHEDULE............. 53
    Contingencies and get-well planning.............. 60
    The Mini-MOST for a sharper focus................ 67
    Bar chart limitations............................ 69
    Keeping change orders under control.............. 71
    MULTIPROJECT SCHEDULING for total control........ 80
    The COUNTDOWN SCHEDULE for systematic completion. 84

3 Winning in Court and Arbitration with MOST.......... 87

    Claims-Consciousness in construction scheduling.. 87
    Six requirements for presentable evidence........ 94

4 MOST as Timely Notice of Damages, Backcharges, and Claims.. 97

    Improvements in performance and
      protection of rights...........................97
    Requirements and advantages of proper notice..... 98
    The notification process......................... 99

THREE

MOST CONTROLS ON RESOURCES TO CUT DIRECT COSTS

5 Simplified Manpower/Cost Management..................111

    Manpower loading......................................112
    Manpower leveling for maximum efficiency.........114

6 MOST/COST for Easy Budgeting and Cost Control.......117

7 Work Performance - Using the Status Index to Relate Actual to Planned Costs.............................123

8 MOST Financial Planning; Maximizing Investment Opportunities and Maintaining Cash-Flow.............127

    Baseline cash-flow projection....................127
    Procedure..129
    Reporting against the baseline cash-flow
       projection; the cumulative/receivable curve....139
    Reporting (plotting) project status..............140
    The status line..................................140
    Reporting (plotting) change orders...............147
    Change order (contract modification) impact......148
    The Maxi-MOST integration........................156
    The status index.................................158

FOUR

LEADERSHIP DEVELOPMENT FOR PERSONAL AND PROFESSIONAL GAIN

9 The MOST Effective Project Leader....................163

    Leadership.......................................163
    The project leader...............................163
    Background of the project leader.................164
    Planning cycle...................................166
    Attributes and failures of leadership............169

10 Controlling Project Administration for Successful Completion and Profit................................173

    Make or buy......................................173
    Project summary..................................173
    The team...175
    Summary..176

Appendix   CPM (Critical Path Method) Scheduling..............179

CONSTRUCTION SCHEDULING SIMPLIFIED

Help

    <u>Construction Scheduling Simplified</u> has been written and arranged in a straightforward, easily understood format. The MOST scheduling technique itself, its principles, and concepts are well within the grasp of busy executives and managers. If, however, for any reason you feel the least bit unsure of materials presented, we will be happy to answer your written questions, addressed to:

    CONSTRUCTION SCHEDULING SIMPLIFIED
    c/o Construction Industry Development Group
    Post Office Box 190
    Bethany, Connecticut 06525

    In addition, consulting services are available at whatever level you may require. Typical arrangements range from individual or group seminars and instruction in the MOST Technique, to providing custom schedules for your individual projects, and updating, or assisting your personnel to update each revision. If you feel confident in applying the MOST Simplified Construction Scheduling System, you may wish to have the schedules for your first one or two projects reviewed before their release. In any of these cases, write to the above address for the current Rate Schedule.

    Finally, we welcome your comments, remarks, and suggestions regarding MOST, <u>Construction Scheduling Simplified</u>, and their presentation, and we look forward to your continued success in the use of this powerful and cost-efficient planning and scheduling capability.

ONE

Simplified Planning, Scheduling, and Control

1
Planning for Profit: The Management Operation System Technique

Intelligent planning, scheduling, and control are absolutely essential to the success of any program: research and development, construction, manufacturing, bids, proposals, etc. The Management Operation System Technique (MOST) invented in 1961, replaces PERT and CPM on construction projects and in program management. Since its inception, MOST has gained popularity and is now widely used in both large and small construction projects. Its use has been equally effective on projects ranging from several thousand dollars to $193 million so far.

Elements of several traditional and modern planning techniques (bar chart, Gantt chart, PERT, CPM, etc.) are combined in this newest management tool, MOST. The advantages of each of these methods have been extracted and the disadvantages of each have been eliminated.

MOST not only contributes to single project R & D, construction, bids, and proposals, but also to Multi-Project Scheduling (MPS) either in production short runs or R & D. MOST's contribution to MPS has added another management tool to help satisfy the ever increasing need for better multi-project scheduling methods.

MOST has been developed to give the project manager visibility; presenting all information necessary for good project control simply and clearly, and in time to allow effective management action. Its early warning system identifies potential trouble areas requiring management action and pin-points long-lead-time tasks. It also provides well-organized data for timely and comprehensive reporting. MOST can be particularly useful in monitoring programs that cross company, division, or department lines, making it an extremely helpful tool for the General Manager. MOST has the added advantage of presenting a graphic picture of a project's status, manpower loading, costs, and any related weak spots in an easily read schedule (often on a single piece of paper).

The use of either CPM or MOST does not guarantee project success. Like any other management tool, they depend on the good judgment, experience, and competence of the people who provide and interpret the data. MOST will free you of the need to continually devote attention to unnecessary details, to allow you to focus your time, energy, and creativity on managing your projects - not just on manipulating data.

THE MOST SIMPLIFIED SCHEDULING TECHNIQUE

When planning a project of any size, CPM can be used, if desired, to establish milestones and estimated times. If CPM is not used, milestones and float (or slack) time become apparent as the MOST schedule begins to take shape. You'll see how float in MOST will be determined <u>without any calculation</u>, such as the forward and backward passes needed in CPM.

If you prefer to use an existing CPM or other computer scheduling method to supply the schedule logic and dependencies, you may continue to do so. In that case, you will simply convert the network diagram into MOST to provide all the benefits to be gained by MOST's unique graphic monitoring capabilities in a schedule that <u>never needs to be redrawn</u>. MOST converts CPM paths into bars keyed to working days, so that progress against scheduled deadlines can be checked easily by project supervisors.

In any case, once MOST is mastered, the planner can go directly to MOST without the use of either CPM or anything else.

Refer to the Appendix for a detailed discussion of the Critical Path Method (CPM).

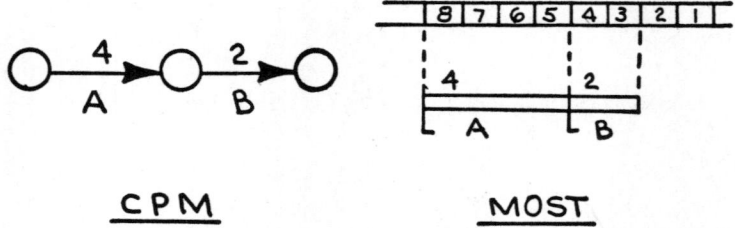

<u>CPM</u>   <u>MOST</u>

A MOST schedule is divided vertically into calendar periods. Programmed activities are displayed as segments of hollow bars, with events appearing as flags at the appropriate time positions along the bars. When two or more paths terminate a single event, only one bar continues along the chart. An arrow is drawn vertically from the tail-end of each discontinued bar to the surviving path, to show the relationship between them.

Thus, a MOST user can see at a glance when a job-and-path is scheduled to begin and end, and what other jobs hinge on its completion. In addition to displaying deadlines, a MOST chart also shows how far a job has actually gone. This is done by a unique method of blocking in the hollow bars. To check progress, a vertical reporting line is placed on the schedule from the calendar scale periodically, to highlight all the activities scheduled to progress as of the reporting date. Bars filled in right up to the reporting lines are on schedule; those filled in short of the line are behind schedule; and those blocked in solidly to a point beyond the reporting line are ahead of schedule.

The MOST schedule differs from PERT and CPM in that when the critical sequence(s) of activities is (are) established, MOST completes the schedule by then working backwards from the contract completion date. But before constructing a MOST schedule, you must first decide on the level of detail required to monitor the program. This will vary, depending upon the size and type of projects being monitored.

Since the schedule is time-oriented, there is less initial effort in preparing the first MOST draft. After the MOST is drawn and coordinated with management and department supervision, actual reporting begins. MOST clearly shows a project's day-to-day status. Critical paths and float times are shown at a glance. The MOST is laid out to show the latest date that a job can start without jeopardizing the schedule.

All the updating is done manually, although the system can feed a computer, should the need arise. But in any case, manually updating MOST will take one hour or _less_, regardless of project size or complexity. This is because reporting centers around those activities to be monitored during the reporting period.

USING MOST FOR CONSTRUCTION

MOST schedules are generally drawn on 22 x 34 inch or 24 x 36 inch paper for standardization. The paper should be reproducible (Vellum) in order to convert to blue prints for normal distribution. The Vellum paper will become the schedule master which can be updated weekly, reproduced and stored. The following figures will illustrate the technique in preparing a MOST schedule.

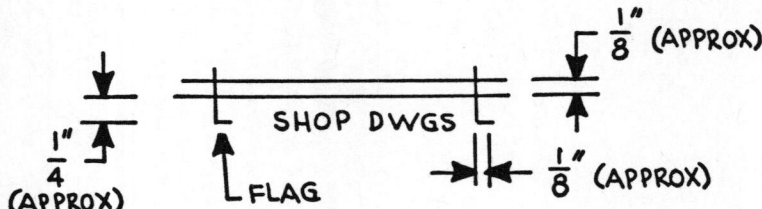

Figure 1-1

The time estimate for shop dwgs., 20 days, is entered immediately above the bar and to the right of the starting flag (see Figure 1-2).

Figure 1-2

In construction schedules, the time estimates are shown in days, not weeks, because that is the language generally used. When applying the calendar to the top of the schedule, the normal calendar (4-1/3 weeks to a month) is used. All of the construction holidays are deleted in order to reflect the normal 40-hour work week, minus holidays (see Figure 1-3).

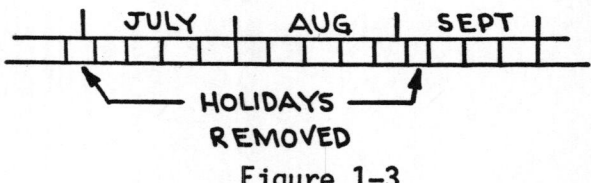

Figure 1-3

Figure 1-4 illustrates the designation of time, and the duration in days.

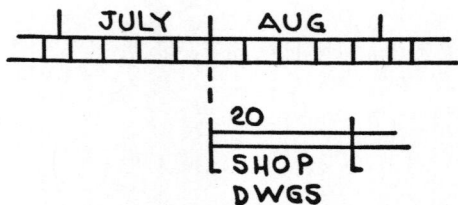

Figure 1-4

As shown in Figure 1-5, jobs can occur in a series, overlap, or be parallel, depending upon their time and project relationships.

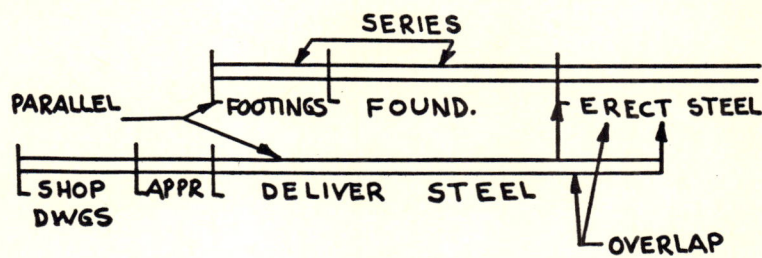

Figure 1-5

The basic MOST schedule (Figure 1-6) includes jobs, delay notes, title block, and trend analysis.

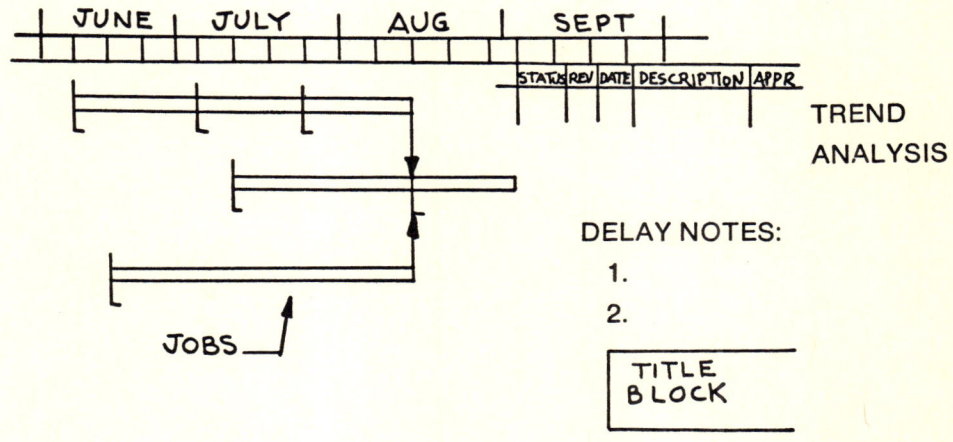

Figure 1-6

MOST vs CPM FOR BETTER UNDERSTANDING

In the Appendix on CPM, a CPM for a dog house (Figure A-6) is shown. Now, to illustrate the conversion to MOST, Figure 1-7 shows the basic directions. Note that the float time in MOST is shown by dash lines in front of the job (with CPM analysis, it is reflected at the back of the job). The estimated times (t_e) are above the bar, and the bar represents the job. The length of the bar matches the duration to the calendar; whereas the length of the job in CPM does not matter (arrow = job in CPM). The flags in MOST are equivalent to events in CPM. The logic and language is the same for CPM and MOST.

32   PLANNING FOR PROFIT: THE MANAGEMENT OPERATION SYSTEM TECHNIQUE

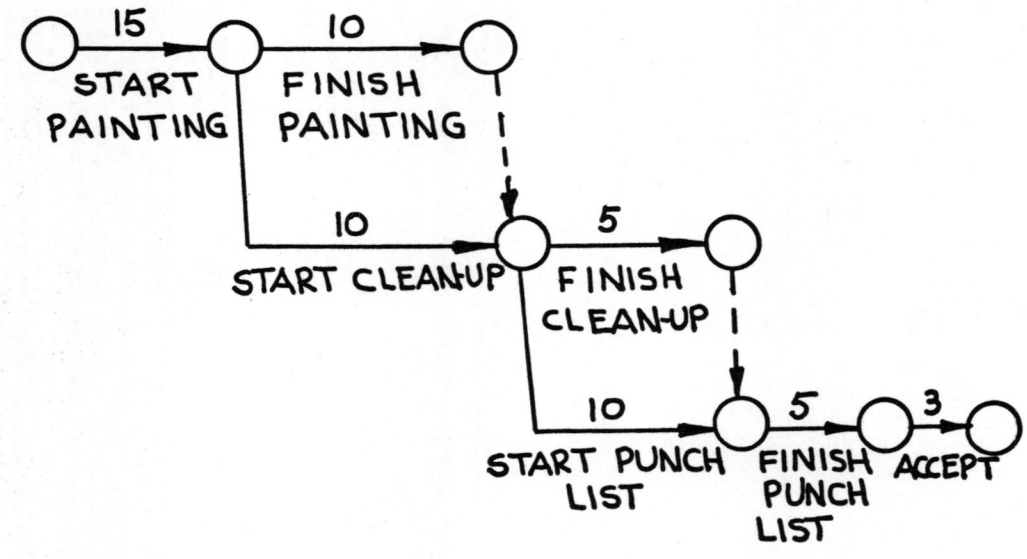

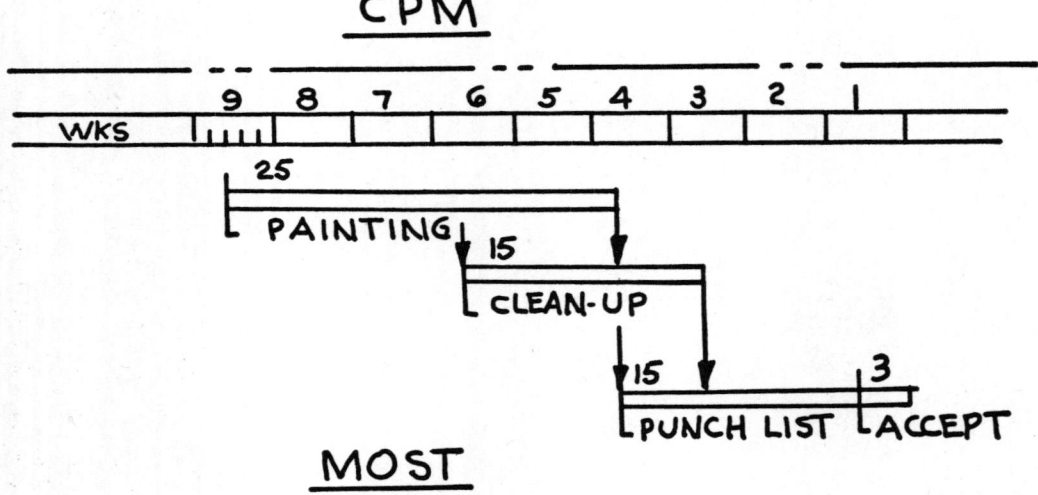

CPM vs. MOST

Figure 1-7

Figure 1-8, on the following page, illustrates the MOST conversion from CPM (figure A-7 in the Appendix); "Small-One Story

PLANNING FOR PROFIT: THE MANAGEMENT OPERATION SYSTEM TECHNIQUE 33

Building". Note that splitting of jobs is illustrated better graphically with MOST than with CPM. For example:

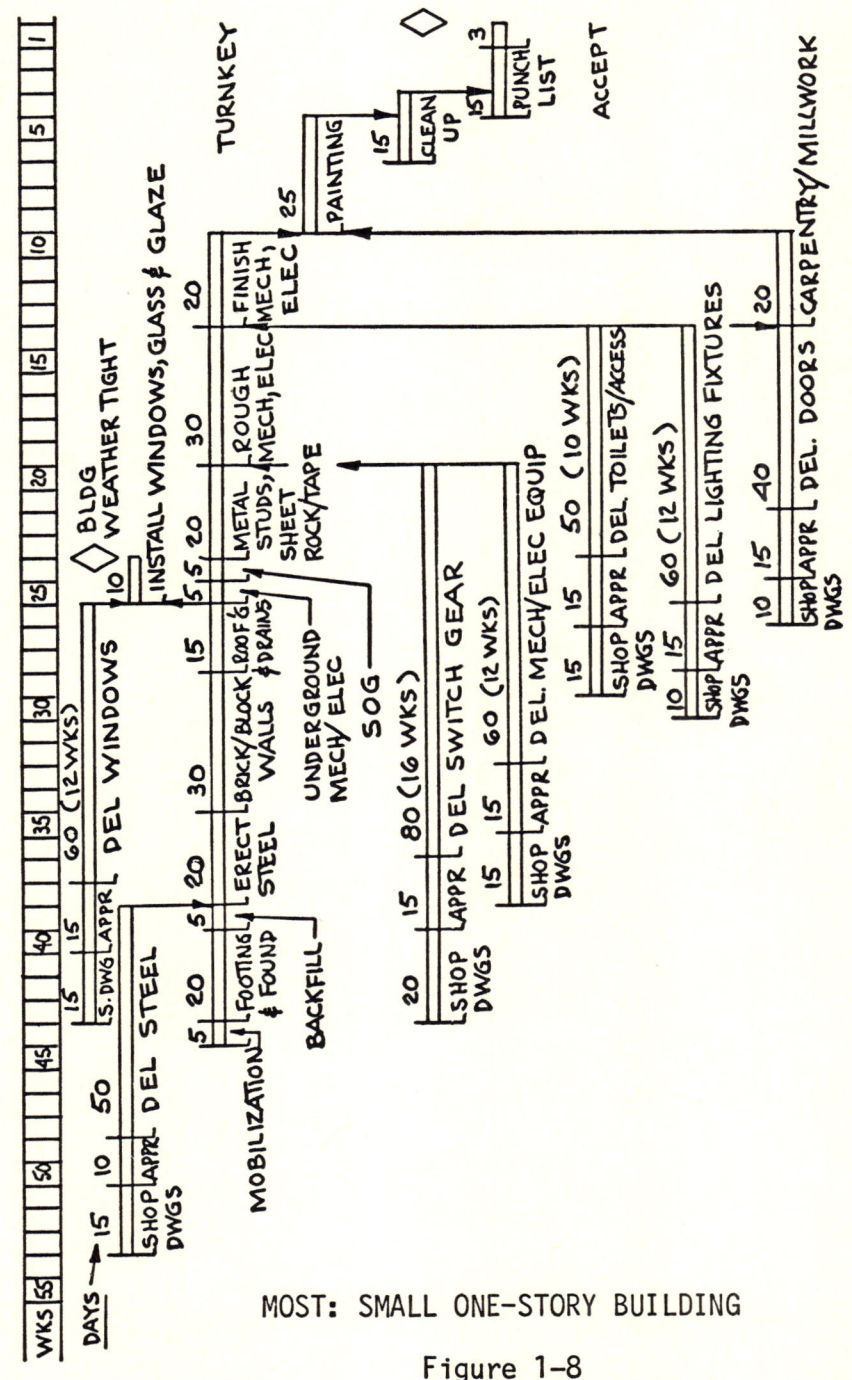

MOST: SMALL ONE-STORY BUILDING

Figure 1-8

THE MOST EASY (ONE HOUR) UPDATE METHOD

A project manager may never realize his or her best intentions because of changing circumstances in the chain of events that leads to successful project completion. With the inception of MOST, the manager now has a long-needed and <u>practical</u> tool to control the project.

MOST projects are successful only if they are completed in the shortest possible time, on time, and are completely thorough. To accomplish these three objectives, the project manager must develop a logical approach in the form of a written plan.

Preparing a detailed schedule forces the user of MOST to think through all possible steps required to complete the project; the user must identify each phase, and recognize and schedule each job. Each step can then be analyzed functionally, and the unneeded ones can be eliminated. In addition, the planner/scheduler can determine the longest (critical) path.

Updating records on a schedule indicates the degree of completion of a project's jobs on a given date. After the planner has obtained job progress status from the planning group member, this information is placed on the schedule as the updating record.

To make the MOST system effective, the schedule must be updated often enough to insure good project control. You, the manager, will decide the frequency of updating. Often, in-house reporting is done weekly, with formal revisions being distributed monthly. If a project is short in duration, is in a critical stage, or is in a problem period, you may elect to monitor and update the schedule on a daily, weekly, or biweekly basis, to give it an appropriate level of attention. A project with a longer duration may need such attention only once each month. You have the flexibility to decide for yourself. Daily or weekly updates with MOST do <u>not</u> mean a lot of extra work, because the process is so quick and <u>easy</u>.

First, the planner asks the team members, subcontractors, and suppliers the following questions to assess the job progress at the updating time:

1. What work has been done?

2. Will a given job in a path meet the schedule?

3. Will the job better the schedule? If so, by how much?

4. Will the job miss the schedule? If so, how much more time is needed?

PLANNING FOR PROFIT: THE MANAGEMENT OPERATION SYSTEM TECHNIQUE

The MOST schedule is updated when the job bars are filled in with tape or pencil to indicate the exact amount of work <u>remaining</u> (in time). As illustrated below, some detailed drawings and some procurement have been completed. Therefore, the bars are filled in. Note, however, that the bars are filled in not to indicate how much time has been spent (as in bar-chart updating), but to show how much time is needed to finish the task.

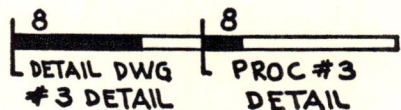

The updating of this plan is done by either a planning specialist, staff administrator, project manager, time keeper at the site, or the superintendent. A successful method is to have the project manager and the site superintendent provide update information from both their locations, and combine the data in the distributed revision. They gather updating information, flag delays, and forecast project completion date. Whether or not a planning specialist is available, the establishment of the MOST function and monitoring job progress will add little to the project cost.

PERCENTAGE OF COMPLETION

Now that the basic requirements have been shown, you can see that the MOST technique really starts with a sophisticated bar-chart in reverse. But what makes this system so unique is the method of updating. Many have found it difficult to update and to get meaningful information from a bar, or Gantt chart, but now, with the technique used in MOST, users can effectively update either bar charts, Gantt Charts, or MOST schedules.

Reporting of percentage completion for each job is not acceptable, because it does not give a true picture of progress relative to time. For example, for a six-week activity, the cognizant person may report at the end of three weeks that it is 50 percent completed.

Now let us analyze this situation. Figure 1-9 shows that at the time of reporting, the progress of the job is on schedule, with three weeks remaining. The important question at this time is: will the

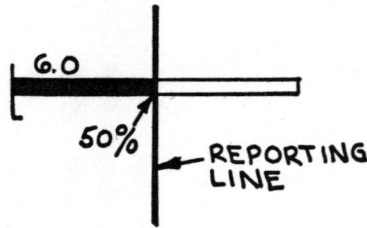

Figure 1-9

job be completed in the remaining three weeks? If the answer is "yes," then it is on schedule as shown. But if the answer is "no," then when will the job be finished? If the job requires five more weeks to complete, will the job be 50 percent complete? With five weeks remaining to finish, the status will show two weeks behind schedule, as in Figure 1-10.

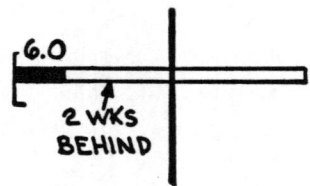

Figure 1-10

The 50%-to-complete may have been the correct "status" with regard to cost and/or physical work in place, but it took one week to accomplish the first 50 percent, and the remaining five weeks to accomplish the second 50 percent. On the other hand, six weeks may have been originally underestimated, or the estimated percentage was only a guess and actual progress was not investigated. If the estimates are the best obtainable and the schedule is firm, actual progress of completion must be fed into the schedule; not the "percentage of completion." To back up status on the schedule fully, the most important question must always be: "When will the activity be completed in relation to the schedule?"

This reasoning has explained the restriction of percentage completion for each job or activity, but MOST can illustrate percentage completion for an entire "planned project or program." Once the plan for a complete project has been established and approved, the project manager can estimate at what point the project can be, say, 50%, 75%, or 80% complete (see Figure 1-11).

An analysis of the updated project (Figure 1-11) shows that the worst condition is two weeks behind schedule. The job ahead of schedule has very little to do with the estimating of completion, since there are some behind schedule. Prorating the behind schedule versus the reporting line, one may judge that the project is 45 percent complete, which means that the project is 5 percent behind schedule. This information can be useful for management, since the MOST schedule can be used as a back-up for this project status report.

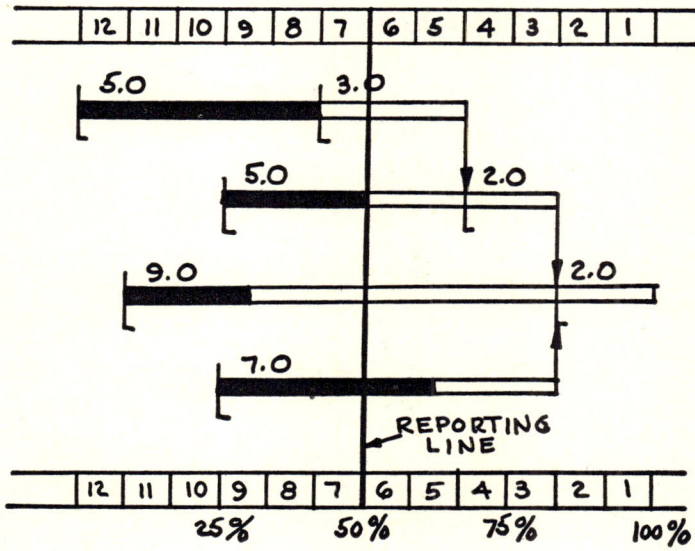

UPDATED PROJECT

Figure 1-11

After the initial MOST schedule is drawn, a copy should be sent to all the subcontractors, architects, engineers, and the owner for their concurrence, since their input is included. Once they have agreed, added new inputs, corrected their original inputs, and have signed off to the final information, the planner will incorporate the latest changes. This updated MOST will now become the BASELINE SCHEDULE from which tracking progress will commence.

As mentioned, the updating of construction MOST should be once per week, whether at the site review meeting, or prior to the meeting. The site superintendent incorporates daily the jobs that were completed, and at the same time updates the copy of MOST that is posted in the field office. Time keepers at the site must be trained to update site jobs on MOST schedules to aid the superintendent. The project engineer or manager will update off-site jobs (deliver switch gear, shop drawings, architect approval, and so on). With both on-site and off-site updated information, MOST can be brought up to date and reissued for site use or use by others on request. It is recomended that the owner receive schedule updates once per month (or more often if there is a serious problem).

When updating the MOST schedules, the job bars will be filled in to show progress. Two questions will be asked: How much time is needed?, and When will the job be completed? With the answers to these questions, one can update MOST to reflect true indications of progress, because the MOST schedule is drawn to show the latest starts. This means that the bars can never be shifted to the left.

In Figure 1-12, "MOST Updating of Dog House," the updating illustrates one day behind schedule. Any white spaces to the left of the reporting line mean behind schedule; any bars filled in up to the reporting line mean on schedule (OS); any bars filled in to the right of the reporting line reflect progress of those activities ahead of schedule. The reporting line is drawn vertically every time status is required. The line moves to the right usually every week, and will illustrate the amount of time to complete the project.

An analysis and evaluation of Figure 1-12 indicates that if the father is responsible for building the frame, he is one day behind schedule, because no updating (or filling in of that bar) was made. But his son has spent at least one day on building the door, and he feels that he will finish the job in two days. All lumber and hardware are in, and shop drawings are completed. In order to finish on time, the father must now "build frame" in the remaining four days. The son feels that he can finish his job in two days; therefore, using the MOST technique to update, you must back off to the left to two remaining days from the activity completion, drop (draw in) the reporting line, and update (fill in the bar) to that line. In this case, it will indicate that this job is one day ahead of schedule

Note that when updating any activity, it will always be the amount of time _remaining_ to complete the particular activity that is left open on the activity bar. This is a significant departure from bar charts (which merely indicate time spent after the fact), most versions of CPM, and many other techniques which use percentage of completion, but which don't properly accomodate the time actually

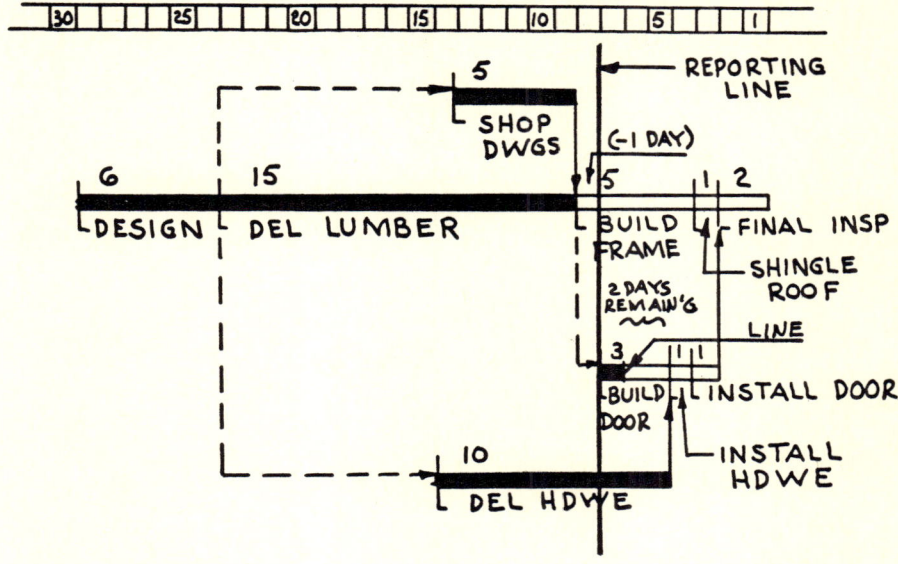

MOST UPDATING OF DOG HOUSE

Figure 1-12

necessary to finish. It is most important for you to recognize that it is the time necessary to finish an activity, rather than the time spent to date on the activity that is most important in reporting status accurately.

To get an idea of MOST updating and the total picture, let's look at Figure 1-13, which shows an industrial assembly.

Expected completion dates are posted at the end of the jobs which are not completed and evolve around the reporting line. "ProcGear" job is expected to be completed on 10/31. This date is three weeks from completion as of the reporting date (indicated by the reporting line). The 10/31 is now backed off from the end of "ProcGear" three weeks to the left, and a mark is placed on the bar. Update (fill in) the bar to this point, and it will reflect that this job is one week behind schedule. Therefore, by knowing the amount of time remaining, the MOST scheduler can visually display this by backing that time off from the end of the job. Without these dates posted, you will not have dates to compare with when updating the next time.

Figure 1-13 shows two weeks behind schedule for "Buy Housing Casting," with eleven weeks to completion of the project. Because of the delay to "Buy Housing Casting," this project is in schedule

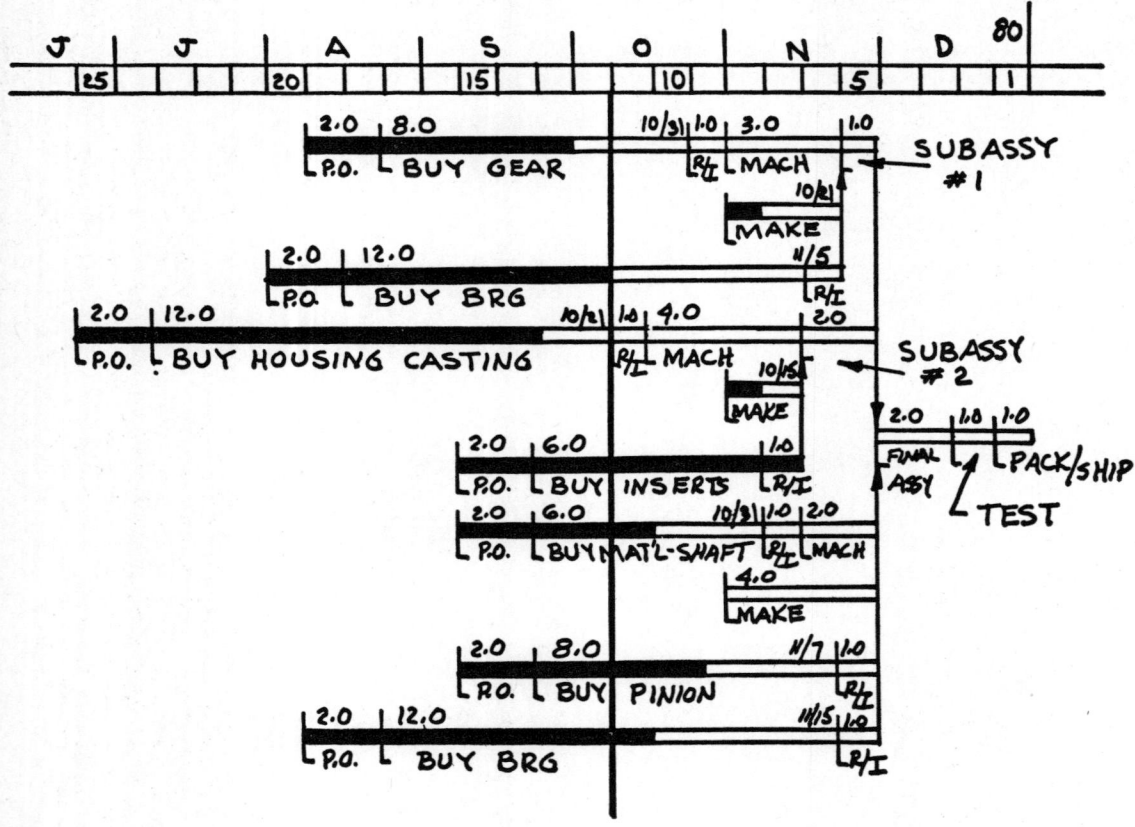

MOST UPDATE OF INDUSTRIAL PROJECT

Figure 1-13

trouble because now the project will take 13 weeks to complete the job needed in the remaining 11 weeks. This dynamic updating technique is unique to MOST, and has revolutionized the updating process not only in construction, but in other businesses as well.

RESCHEDULING WITHOUT REDRAWING WITH MOST

After the preliminary MOST schedule has been issued for review, comments, corrections, or new input, one week should be allowed for feedback to update MOST and establish the Baseline Schedule, from which tracking can begin. ("Tracking" is monitoring the status of a project, preferably on a weekly basis.) During the times of

PLANNING FOR PROFIT: THE MANAGEMENT OPERATION SYSTEM TECHNIQUE

monitoring the construction jobs, there are bound to be extended or reduced times evident, new jobs added to the schedule, or any of an infinite number of changes and effects that will cause slippages or extended schedules. The MOST system is developed to account for these problems without redrawing, or preparing a completely new schedule for each update (as is necessary with CPM). This approach at the onset may appear impossible, but MOST is probably the only system that can accomplish a no-redraw at every update. With this approach, MOST will retain history and easily clarify the usually complicated project record. These advantages will prove to be invaluable during any subsequent settlements, court litigations, and arbitrations (this will be explained in detail later).

Figure 1-14 below will begin to illustrate the no-redraw technique.

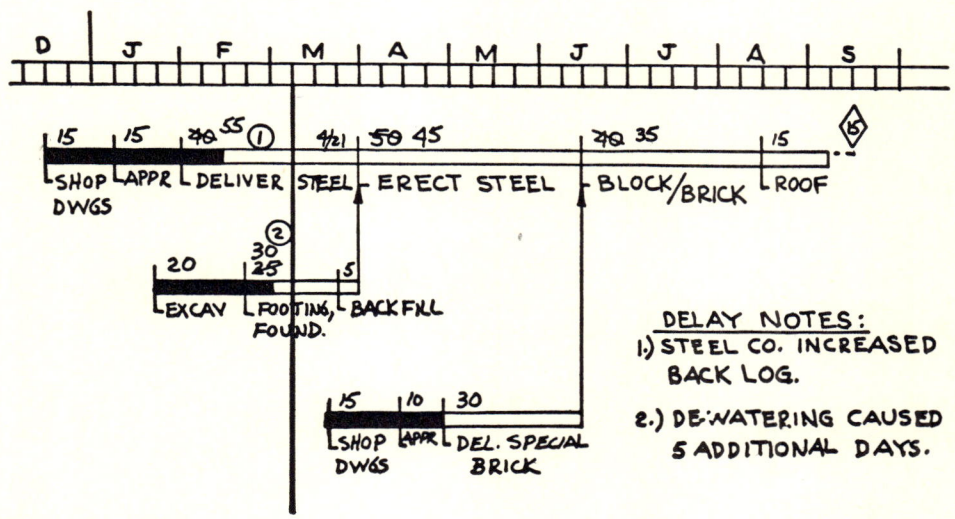

RESCHEDULING WITHOUT REDRAWING

Figure 1-14

In beginning to analyze Figure 1-14, note the reporting line shown on March 7th. The job "Deliver Steel" shows a 4/21 date to be on the site, as compared to the planned date of April 1st as indicated by the end of the activity bar as originally drawn. The difference between 4/21 and the reporting line (3/7) is five weeks. To show progress, you back off five weeks from the end of "Deliver

Steel" (moving to the left), mark the bar, and update to that mark. It immediately becomes evident that the job is three weeks behind schedule (note that all white spaces to the left of the reporting line indicate those activities to be behind schedule by the respective amounts).

This extension of the required time also changes the delivery lead time from the planned (scheduled) 40 days to 55 days. The "40 days" will be lined out but _not removed_ for historical purposes. The job "Footings & Foundations" also slipped (5 days), and the same procedure is used to show progress and status. The important question again is: How much more time is _remaining_? This amount of time remaining is shown as the hollow portion of the job bar to show true indication of progress.

Now that the MOST schedule reflects project completion to be three weeks behind schedule, what are we going to report to our superiors, and how will we get back on schedule, pick up time, get well, or work around?

A glance down stream in the schedule reflects reduced times for "Erect Steel" and "Block/Brick." The schedule is not redrawn; the elapsed times are changed, but not the bar. Therefore, two of the three weeks have been picked up graphically, and the remainder is not picked up. This means that the end job or path is now extended one week to 9/15. This indicates that as of March 7 the project is three weeks behind schedule, yet the get-well plan indicates that two weeks can be picked up, leaving a one week extension if the 45 days and the 35 days respectively are good estimates, and are completed with these new inputs. Then the 50 day and the 40 day bars are filled in. We do not change the bars because there is always some possibility that the job may revert back to original estimates.

As the reporting line moves to the right, and if the one week extended is picked up, the 9/15 date will be lined out. The name of the construction game is to keep on schedule. Delay notes appear in the area of behind schedule (1, 2), and are referenced and identified in the "Delay Notes" column. This clarifies and illustrates the "Why behind schedule" and where this occurs. These delay notes and symbols are never removed and will appear on all subsequent schedule revisions.

Figure 1-15 illustrates the reporting line moved to the end of March, and "Deliver Steel" continues to slip for the same reason. In rescheduling without redrawing, you continue to change estimated times and line out previously posted time changes, also, the subsequent jobs are again analyzed and adjusted. With four weeks behind schedule at this update time, only two weeks can be picked up, and the project completion date is extended two weeks. The rationale is the same as in Figure 1-12. In this manner, the "why behind," "where it occurred," and "extension in the project completion date" can be used to the general contractor's advantage if litigation or arbitration is forthcoming.

If the project leader keeps and files all revisions of MOST schedule updates, the progress performed between revisions can be seen. The MOST technique provides for this other dynamic visibility. A look at Figure 1-15.A illustrates a dashed line indicating progress between the update in figure 1-14 and the update in Figure 1-15. Because a copy of the current schedule revision is used as the worksheet in preparation of the next schedule update, in practice the dashed line in the Figure may take the form of red pencil as the scheduler modifies the previous revision.

The dashed line will become solid when revision beyond March 31 is performed, and new progress will become a dashed line. This technique is also beneficial to the general contractor if partial or percentage payments have been negotiated.

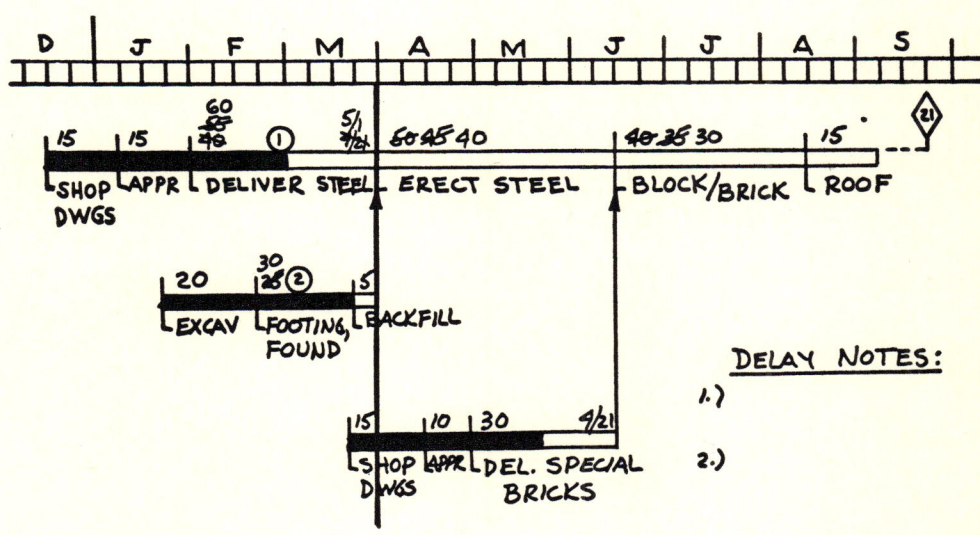

RESCHEDULING WITHOUT REDRAWING

Figure 1-15

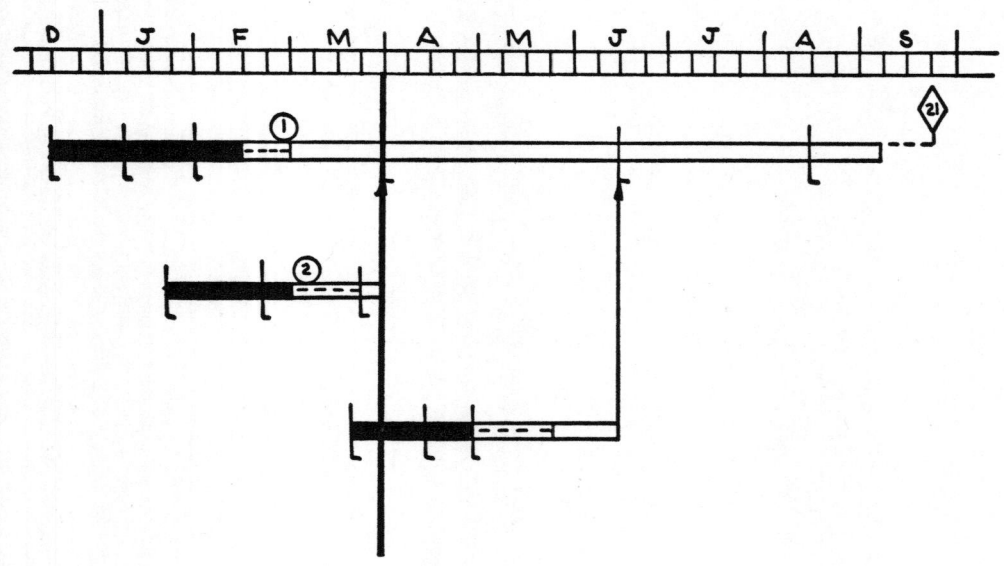

PROGRESS UPDATE

Figure 1-15.A

SCHEDULE ANALYSIS AND EVALUATION

Once construction schedules are tracked, monitored, and reported weekly, the project leader or scheduler may want to prepare a schedule analysis to evaluate the current status, associated problems, if any, and alert the front office management to where the project is heading. The analysis can then be stored in the project file for historic records. Many project engineers write extensive and wordy accounts of the current project status which adds unnecessary information to the project file. Simpler information at their finger tips would facilitate this effort. When CPM is used and a computer is required, the feedback is often lagging in time for immediate reporting. Discussed below is a simple visual information technique which will reduce time in accumulating data, and shorten the writing effort.

The Trend Analysis approach shown in Figure 1-16 will appear on all MOST schedules. Whenever the MOST is updated, the current status in days will appear in the Status column. If the project is on schedule, a "0" will appear. When behind schedule 5 days, a "-5 D" will be posted. When ahead of schedule by 5 days, a "+5 D" will appear. Each weekly update will be represented by a letter in the Revision column, and its date shown in the Date column. The reason

STATUS	REV	DATE	DESCRIPTION	APPR
0	A	9-1-78	INITIAL RELEASE	ALI
-5D	B	9-8-78	SHOP DWGS-STEEL	ALI
-10	C	9-15-78	STEEL DWG APPROVAL	ALI
-15 / -10	D	9-22-78	LATE RELEASE STEEL ORDER DEWATER	ALI
-8	E	10-1-78	COMPLETE DEWATER	ALI

TREND ANALYSIS

Figure 1-16

for the status time will be explained briefly in the Description column (such as delay footings, lack of shop drawings, or awaiting window and door HM frames), and appropriate records referenced as back-up. Generally, the project engineer initials the revision in the Approval column.

As updating status continues to reflect increasing negative float, this indicates that whatever the problems, they are either not getting attention, or circumstances beyond their control need time to be corrected. The name of the scheduling game is to try to get back on schedule as soon as possible. In the construction business, it is very unnatural to pick up a bulk of negative float. It seems likely that one day negative float may be realized during a two-week work span.

The Schedule Analysis and Evaluation Report, Figure 1-17, is a way to notify either the owner or the front office management of various bits of information that will keep them abreast of where the project is, what causes the problems, what will be done to correct them, and what will be accomplished before the next schedule update. In item #2 of this report, only one of the three lists will be answered. Usually, this report is filled out monthly and the information for the nine questions will be transferred from the updated MOST schedule.

These monthly schedule analyses and evaluation reports should be completed with all MOST revisions. These records can also be used in litigation and arbitration.

PLANNING FOR PROFIT: THE MANAGEMENT OPERATION SYSTEM TECHNIQUE

SCHEDULE ANALYSIS AND EVALUATION REPORT

1. Contract Date and Number:

2. Status to Contract Date:

3. List those jobs that cause slippage(s):

4. Reason(s) for slippage(s):

5. Get Well Plan, or when it will be available:

6. Best estimate to complete (your best judgement):

7. Your confidence in meeting the schedule per updated information:

8. Open items for owner's, subcontractors', or general contractor's attention and action:

9. What to expect to accomplish before the next schedule update:

Figure 1-17

The Variance Report, Figure 1-18 on the following page, is a valuable tool for the project leader to alert not only the owner and construction management, but all the subcontractors and general contractors as well. This report is a vital technique used at project reviews, because important status for all can be reviewed and put on the table for all to negotiate. This technique has proven very valuable in many construction projects where a detailed schedule is available and can be updated further.

These schedule analyses and evaluation techniques have aided many in construction project management in reducing data and paperwork to a minimum to save space in the project file. Whenever there is a method to reduce time, paper, and unnecessary effort in schedule reporting, construction management welcomes this type of advice.

Important and major milestones should be included in the Variance Report. It is advisable to include some milestones that will cover all subcontractors, the owner, and the design professionals. This information will not only help to make a balanced Variance Report, but will insure that all parties to the contract will remain a spoke on the squeaky wheel that gets the most attention. Additional milestones should be added to this report as the work progresses.

ITEM NO	JOB	PLANNED DATE	STATUS 7-1-79	EXPECT'D DATE	STATUS 8-1-79	EXPECT'D DATE	STATUS 9-1-79	EXPECT'D DATE			SHT. 1 OF __
1	COMPL. FOUND	7-16-79	+2 D	7-12-79	COMPL	—	—	—			
2	DEL. STEEL	7-13-79	-5	7-20-79	-14D	8-2-79					
3	SHOP DWG APPR. SWITCHGEAR	6-25-79	-10	7-10-79	COMPL.	—	—	—			
4	SHOP DWG/APPR HM WINDOW FRAMES	6-1-79	-24	7-6-79	COMPL	—	—	—			
5	BACKFILL	8-7-79	—	—	0	8-7-79					
6	START STEEL ERECTION	7-25-79	—	—	-6D	8-6-79					
7	START DRAINAGE SYS	7-18-79	—	—	-16D	8-8-79					
8	ORDER SWITCH GEAR - DEL DATE	11-27-79	—	—	0	11-27-79					
9	ORDER HM WINDOW FRAMES	8-31-79	-6 D	9-11-79	-6	9-11-79					
10											

VARIANCE REPORT

Figure 1-18

TWO

Construction Scheduling Made Easy

2
The MOST Action Program for Project Control

Now that we've covered the basics of MOST, let's focus our attention on the use of MOST, its advantages, simplicity, and visibility in construction. Using MOST for construction is generally easier than for other industries and businesses, mainly because the job titles are the same or similar, time estimates are firm (not fluid), and the cooperation from all who contribute schedule information is better and on time. This chapter, then, will begin to explore the practical construction of MOST and its use as a management tool.

PREPARATION OF THE BASELINE SCHEDULE

Whether a schedule is needed prior to receiving an award, or within a certain time after an award, or even submitted as part of a bid package, the schedule must be responsive to the bid package requirements. This is necessary to assure that the length of time allowed to complete the project is in fact attainable. The necessary scheduling data will come from the team members, such as: the general contractor, superintendent, subcontractors (mechanical, electrical, HVAC, structural steel, masons, etc.), estimators, and construction management. Once all have reviewed the construction plans and specifications, a meeting of the team should be held prior to the start of activities at the designated site. The meeting will only cover those activities pertinent to schedule information. Often, this may be the first meeting of all the team members. The scheduling inputs may therefore necessitate splinter meetings which will be most helpful in better understanding and exchange of important data among members of the team.

The first meeting may last up to two hours, depending upon the arrival of the team members. Be sure that the plans and specifications are available. The person in charge and responsible for the schedule (project engineer, project manager, or scheduler) may lead the meeting and ask scheduling information from one party at a time. When this person has answered the necessary information, it may be helpful to have him or her remain at the meeting in the event that his or her input may be useful in planning or coodinating subsequent activities. It must be understood that this first meeting will only be for collection of scheduling activities, activity times (durations), and relevant dependencies. A preliminary schedule will then be prepared for the team members to review, comment on, and approve.

Allow one week for the team members to return their preliminary copies with or without changes or comments. Once all the inputs have been returned, the scheduler will correct the preliminary schedule and reissue it as the final Baseline Schedule, with or without the team members' signatures (optional). Our preference is to have those who contributed to the schedule sign for their company to acknowledge that the Baseline Schedule is realistic, properly shows interdependencies, and is attainable. Their signatures will confirm that their final inputs are incorporated in the schedule, and that they are satisfied with the overall document. These confirmations will be invaluable if claims or backcharges pop up during the life of the project.

The Baseline Schedule is the final schedule; it is the one that will start the project, the one that will not be redrawn (except in the most extreme delay and/or interference cases), and the one that will represent the project not only for the team members, but for the owner and the design professionals as well. Weekly schedule updates will apply to the Baseline Schedule.

Weekly updates are recommended and should be posted in the site trailer. If team members request these weekly updates, they may certainly receive copies as well. When MOST is first being implemented by your company, it might be useful to have your project field people submit their weekly updates to you, mainly to give your people the message that you mean weekly, and procrastination cannot be tolerated. In any case, if new updates are available in the trailer weekly, the team members can observe and review them at the periodic job-site meetings. An updated copy of the MOST schedule should be available at the general contractor's or construction manager's office, and will, of course, become part of the permanent job record. Finally, the MOST update review should be consistently placed in a prominent position on every job meeting agenda (refer to the detailed discussion on schedule review and distribution in Chapter 4 of this section ("MOST as timely notice...").

One of the key milestones in construction scheduling is weathertighting a building. The following steps are the scheduling considerations to meet this important milestone. Once approval for a go-to-start has been given at the site, "baselines & benchmark," "survey and layout," "install temporary facilities" (electric, phone, etc.) and any miscellaneous jobs needed prior to the physical start of the beginning activity are accounted for in terms of time necessary to complete. Barring unusual circumstances, one week is normally allowed for mobilization. Next, if a project has a basement, for example, extensive excavation may be necessary prior to digging for footings. When referring to footings, this, then, may include excavating, forming and pouring, unless specific characteristics of those activities warrant individual attention. The level of detail in the specific activities used and what they actually include is up to you: whatever makes sense. Next, for this first example, in most buildings, foundations are poured to a particular level. This includes forming, pouring, curing, and removing forms.

We'll now refer to a typical job listing and its lead times from "Construction of Small One Story Building" from Figure A-7 in the Appendix, the activity list for which is reproduced as Figure 2-1 on the following page.

CONSTRUCTION
Small One Story Building

		DAYS
1.	Mobilization	5
2.	Footings/Foundations	20
3.	Backfill	5
4.	Steel — Shop Dwgs, Appr., Del.	15, 15, 50
5.	Erect Steel	20
6.	Brick/Block Walls	30
7.	Roofing/Drains	15
8.	Window — Shop Dwgs, Appr., Del.	15, 15, 60
9.	Install Windows, Glass & Glaze	10
10.	Underground Mech/Elec.	5
11.	SOG	5
12.	Metal Stds, Sheet Rock, Tape	20
13.	Rough Mech/Elec.	30
14.	Switch Gear — Shop Dwgs, Appr., Del.	20, 15, 80
15.	Mech. Equip — Shop Dwgs, Appr., Del.	15, 15, 60
16.	Finish Mech/Elec.	20
17.	Toilets/Access — Shop Dwgs, Appr. Del.	15, 15, 50
18.	Lighting Fixture — Shop Dwgs, Appr. Del.	10, 15, 60
19.	Carpentry/Millwork	20
20.	Doors — Shop Dwgs, Appr., Del.	10, 15, 40
21.	Painting (Int)	25
22.	Clean-up	15
23.	Punch List	15
24.	Acceptance	3

TYPICAL JOB LISTING

Figure 2-1

We'll begin by scheduling the first few activities in Figure 2-2. In this example, backfilling includes dampproofing inside and outside of foundation, installation of perimeter insulation prior to

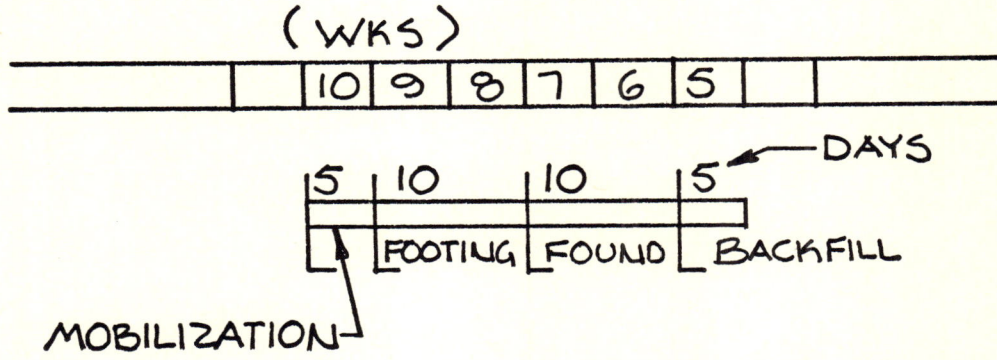

CONTINUE JOB LISTING

Figure 2-2

placing dirt against the foundation. If steel erection is necessary, it will follow or parallel backfilling. Assuming twenty (20) days estimate for steel erection, we must consider what other jobs must be accomplished before steel erection, and back off to the left from the

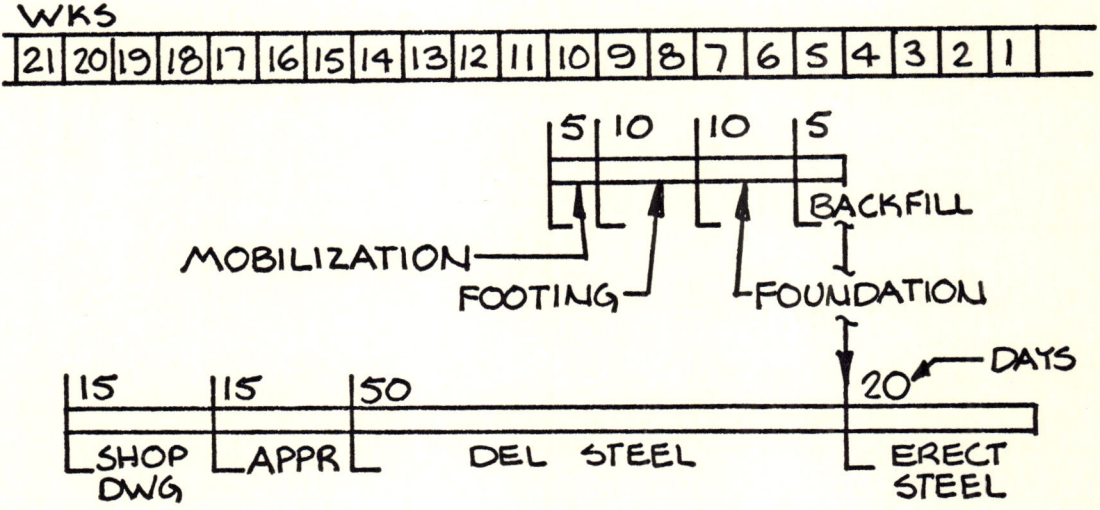

CONTINUE JOB LISTING

Figure 2-3

start of the activity. These items will include shop drawings for steel, architect approval, fabrication of steel members, and delivery to the jobsite. The schedule now begins to take shape, but illustrates a new constraint, as shown in Figure 2-3.

A look at the above illustration discloses a serious but common dilemma: shop drawings for steel should begin at ten weeks prior to mobilization at the site. This presents a significant constraint, because if this schedule were not prepared well in advance, the real critical path might be misdirected.

Some in the construction business ask, "How do I start a schedule?" A look at the examples above shows that when starting with mobilization, one must first ask: "what do I do before this job takes place?" (such as deliver steel before erection of the steel - a constraint activity or job).

In construction scheduling with MOST for a conventional building, proceed from "Mobilization" to the installation of the windows (and then to caulking and sealants, depending upon the desired level of detail), which is normally considered the point at which the building is weathertight. As you proceed, decide what is needed prior to each job and move to the left to define and illustrate the necessary constraints, as shown in Figure 1-8, on page 33. For example, prior to installing windows, openings may require field measuring, the windows must be fabricated, and then delivered. Therefore, schedule "Deliver Windows," "Appr.," and "Shop Drawings" to the left of "Install Windows," to show the latest start date of "Shop Drawings." In addition, to start "Rough Elect" in Figure 1-8, "Switchgear" is needed. By scheduling all the lead times for this job to the left, it becomes apparant that 115 days are required: 20 days for "Shop Drawings," 15 days for "Appr.," and 80 days (16 weeks) for "Fab./Del. Switchgear."

By using the MOST system as described above, the scheduler will develop a realistic schedule. It will not only show what jobs are necessary to erect a building to satisfy weathertighting, but it will also illustrate the latest start of all constraint jobs so as not to jeopardize the schedule or the contract date.

A look at a partial schedule, Figure 2-4, illustrates a high-rise apartment building being erected using pre-fab structures including exterior walls, floors, and curtain walls. Preassembled kitchen and toilet units are also included. This building can have many floors with similar construction for each floor. To illustrate the floor-to-floor relationship, a constraint line after "Erect 1st Floor Structure" continues down to start of "Erect 2nd Floor Structure." This method will continue to the last floor and then to the roofing.

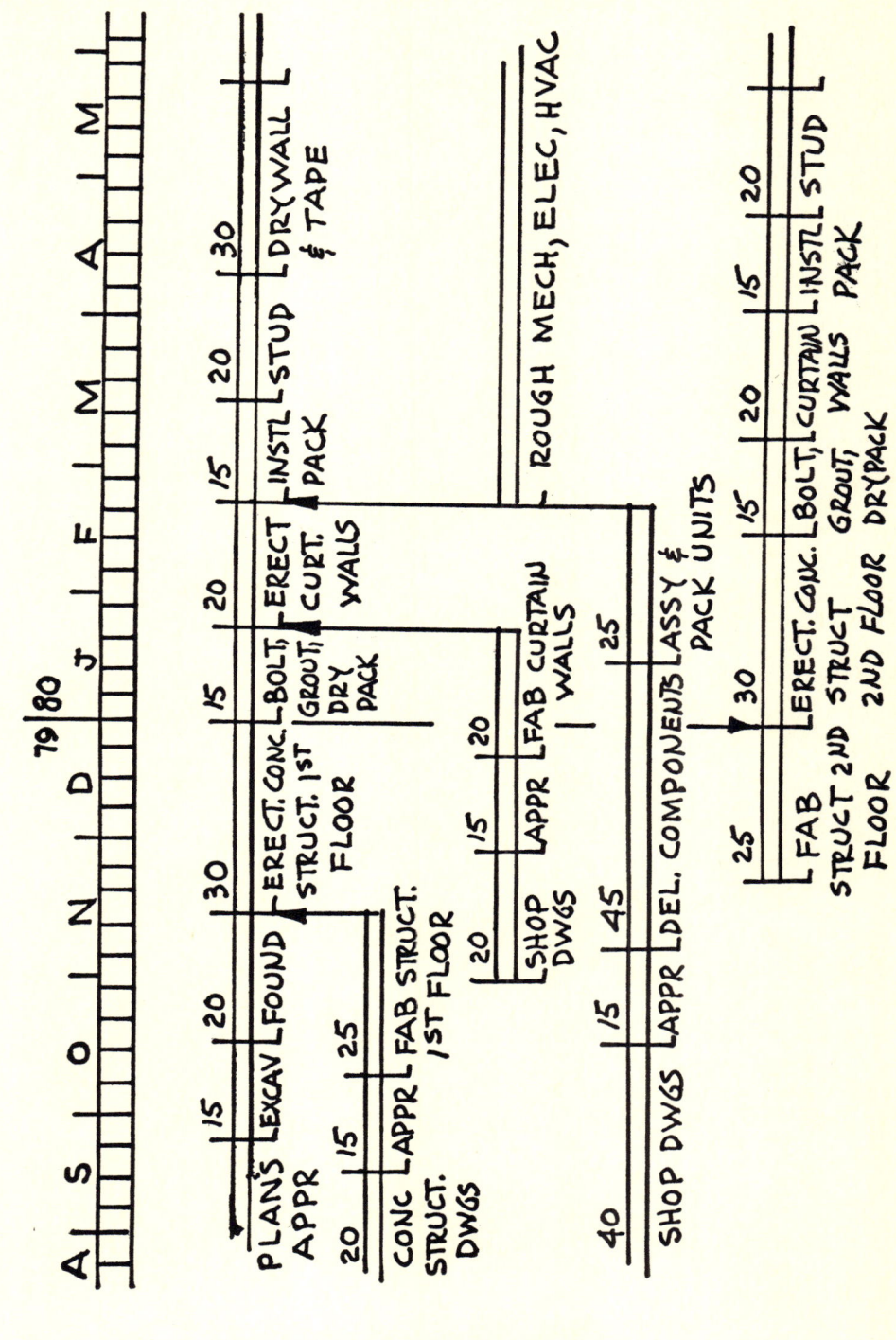

HIGH RISER APARTMENT

Figure 2-4

All other jobs will be shown in their respective schedule positions to clearly display the relationship of parallel and overlapping jobs. If the start up of jobs illustrates too many of the same type of jobs or trades in parallel, the MOST visibility will highlight this potential problem.

Figure 2-4 shows a "success-oriented" schedule. In other words, all jobs must be completed on time within the time frame against the calendar; there is no room for error. There is also no free time to allow for down time or inclement weather. Since construction is most often dependent upon the weather, it is advisable to allow for at least two days per month during the winter months for contingencies or down time. During the spring or summer months, allow one (1) day per month for rain. In many instances, some schedulers may allow two to three weeks per year for inclement weather. It is important to allow for these contingencies when preparing the Baseline Schedule.

CONTINGENCIES AND GET-WELL PLANNING

Let's review Figure 2-4 again and incorporate some contingency times. We will assume for our illustration that this project is being constructed in a cold region; for instance, New England. Mid-December through March are cold and snowy months. Snow, ice, or rain will generally hamper exterior work. If the building is not weathertight during these months, gypsum wallboard, taping, and other finishes cannot commence unless money is spent on temporary heat. Therefore, it may be advantageous to plan installing gypsum wallboard, taping, and subsequent finishes after March 15 (if possible) to avoid unnecessary heat costs.

Since "Erect Structure 1st Floor" is scheduled to be completed some time at the end of December, "Bolt, Grout, and Drypack" in January, and "Erect Curtain Walls" to be completed sometime at the end of February, the following adjustments, as shown in Figure 2-5 on the next page, can be made to the MOST schedule. This is a legitimate schedule move.

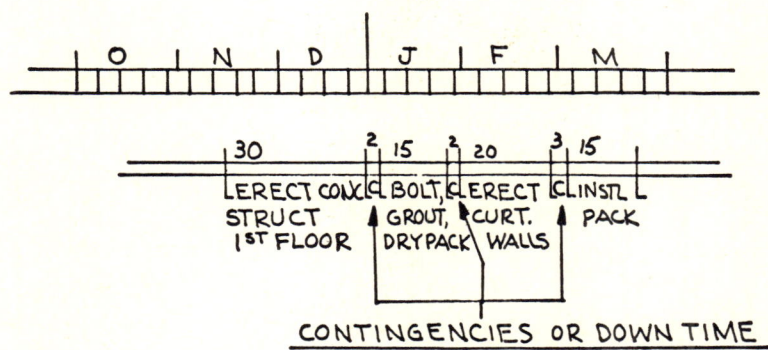

CONTINGENCIES OR DOWN TIME

Figure 2-5

Note that the seven days added for contingencies in the above example are scheduled after the overall baseline schedule has been established. This additional time must be calculated into the schedule and the schedule end date must be responsive to the project contract completion date. In some instances, in an effort to keep the MOST schedule simple, contingency time may be included as part of the total activity time estimate ("Erect Curtain Walls" in Figure 2-5 would then be shown as 23 days). There is nothing wrong with this approach, as long as everyone involved is aware of and recognizes the duration for what it really is. In any case, when all the above has been agreed to, the MOST schedule can now be used to track the project progress. Figure 2-6, then, shows an update in mid-December.

The update at mid-December shows 15 days behind schedule for "Deliver Components for Pack," and 10 days behind schedule for "Erect Conc. Structure for 1st Floor." The remaining jobs are either on schedule or ahead of schedule. This project is in trouble, and the scheduler will show it as such in order that everyone concerned is aware of the criticality, or behind schedule, in time to do something about it. It is important to display all slippages and delays completely and honestly to avoid suffering the consequences before it is too late to correct.

Now that we have shown slips of 15 days and 10 days, we also want

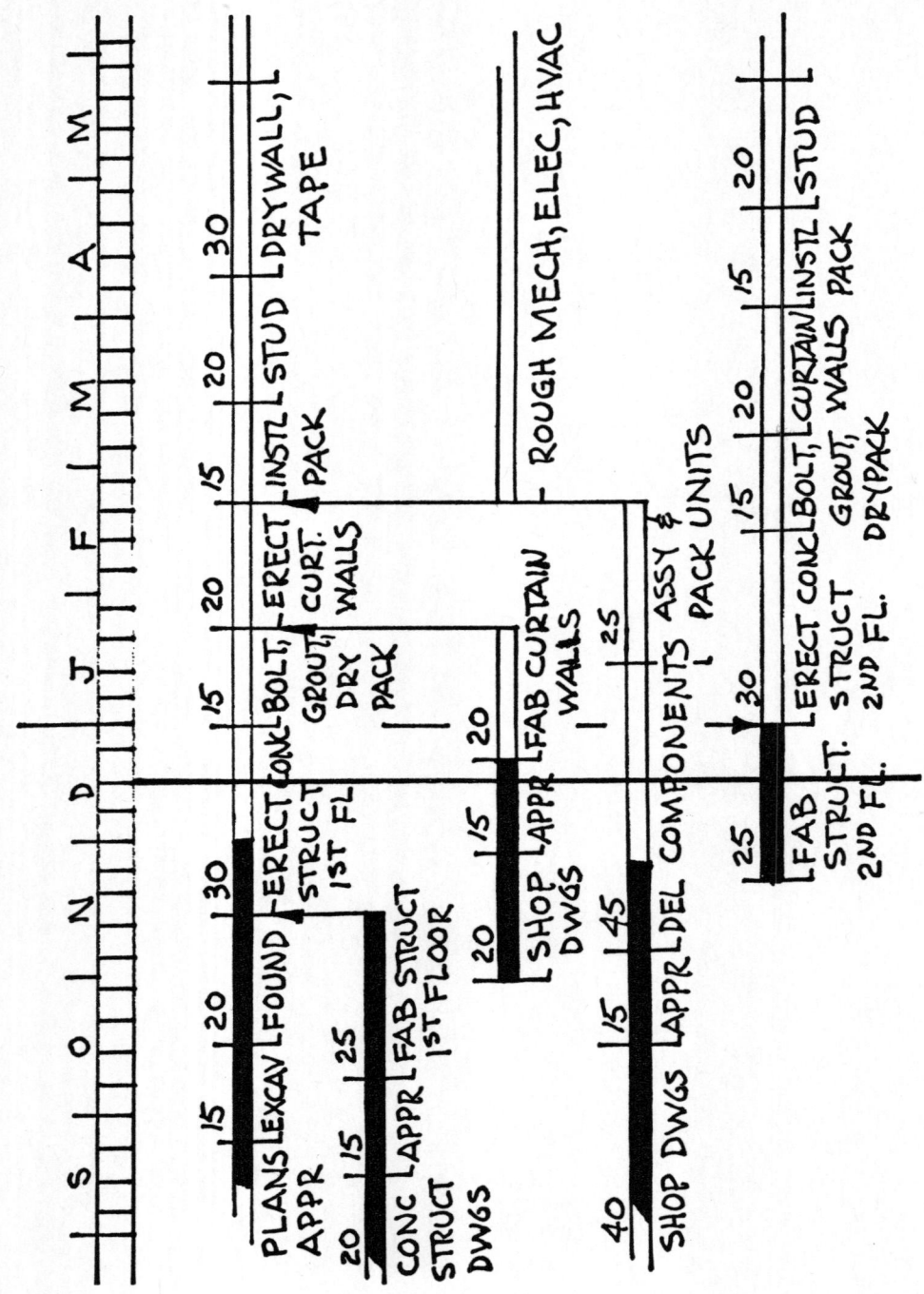

HIGH RISER APARTMENT – UPDATE

Figure 2-6

THE MOST ACTION PROGRAM FOR PROJECT CONTROL 63

to know the reasons why these activities are behind. The use of the "Delay Notes" 1 and 2 will serve this purpose and retain the history. These notes will become very valuable down stream if litigation or arbitration is necessary. The Delay Notes will always remain on the MOST schedule, and will appear as record on all subsequent MOST revisions.

We have reviewed the slippages, the reasons for the slippages, and who has slipped. Now what are we going to do to get back on schedule? What will be our work-around or get-well plan? After a review of the subsequent jobs along those paths that have negative float, we must decide where, by how much, and how the scheduled negative paths can get-well. We must reschedule without redrawing, and show instant visibility.

Figure 2-6 illustrates how some of this negative float can be realized at this update. As project updating continues, hopefully most, or all, of the time will be overcome to get back on schedule in time to finish the project on time.

The get-well plan in Figure 2-7 does not reflect many days of improvement. In the construction business, only a few days of time can be picked up. The path of -15 days reflects an improvement of 5 days realized in the "Job Assembly and Pack Units"; the 25 planned days is now estimated to be complete in 20 days. This reduction may require more people and resources to reduce time. Also, the time in "Install Pack" has been reduced from 15 to 12 days. Again, more labor and equipment may be required. The path of -10 days has been changed. This path interrelates with the other path at "Install Packs." There are 4 days along the -10 day path, and 5 days along the -15 day path, and including the 3 days improvement in "Install Pack," 8 days of the "-15 days" can be picked up at this updating time.

It must be emphasized that the planned times and durations be lined out, but <u>not removed</u>, and the bars remain as is. These planned times and durations remain on the schedule as the updating line moves, to continue to show all slips and improvements relative to planned progress. If the improvements hoped for in the "get-well plan" do not occur, the MOST schedule will revert back to the original plan. All this history - the problems, attempts at improvements, corrections, and so on - will be retained to clarify the official project record.

When reporting the above status, it must be reported that the project is 15 days late as of 12/15, but also that the get-well plan will pick up 8 days to reflect a net slip of only 7 days. The schedule will continue to be worked and massaged, as reporting

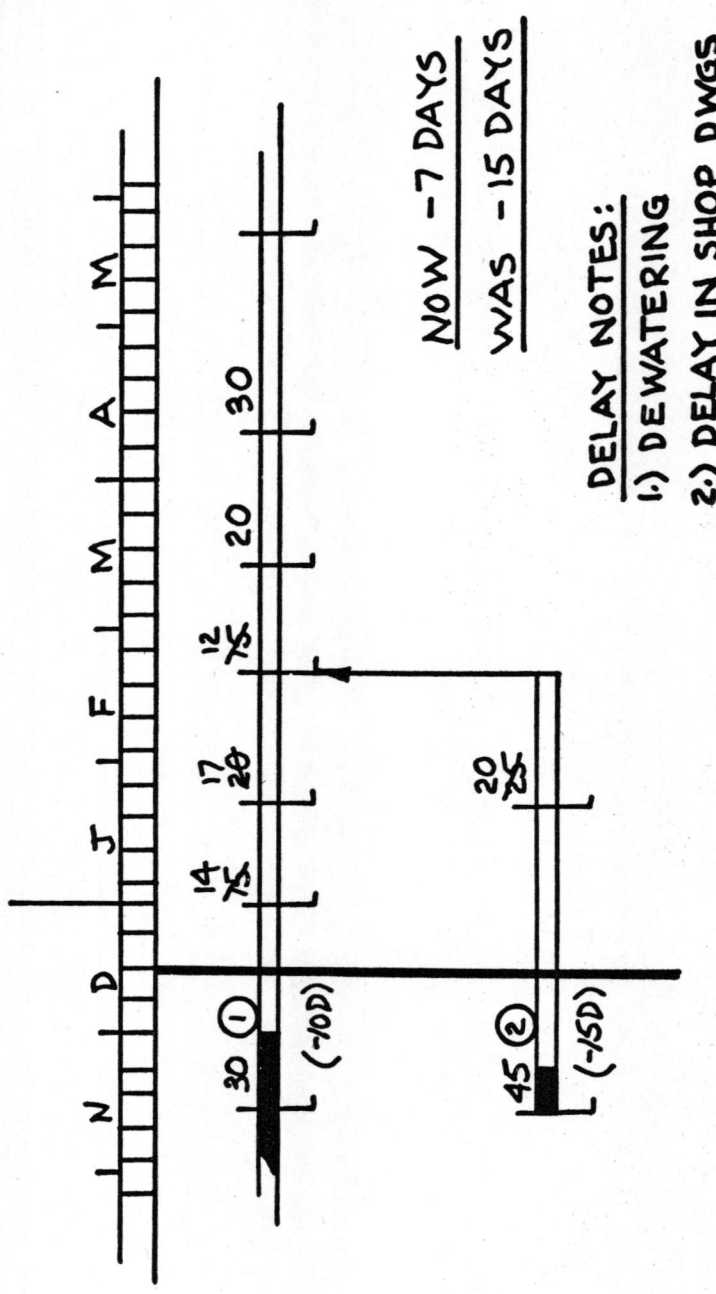

GET-WELL PLAN

Figure 2-7

continues. It is hoped that in the remaining 5 months the
project will be back on schedule. The remaining necessary schedule
data will be included in the Schedule Analysis and Evaluation Report.

Let's now return to Figure 1-8 and add the remaining jobs which
will complete the MOST schedule for this one-story building such as
site work, additional subcontractors' jobs, and others. Figure 2-6
is a complete MOST schedule with contingencies built-in. If we make
this our Baseline Schedule, we can now commence tracking progress
weekly. A copy of all revisions should be kept on file until the
project is completed, all payments have been received and made, and
all required waivers and releases obtained. It is also recommended
that the original reproducible vellum be stored in the event a
similar project is bid at a later date. This schedule will then be
of some use if a bid schedule is required.

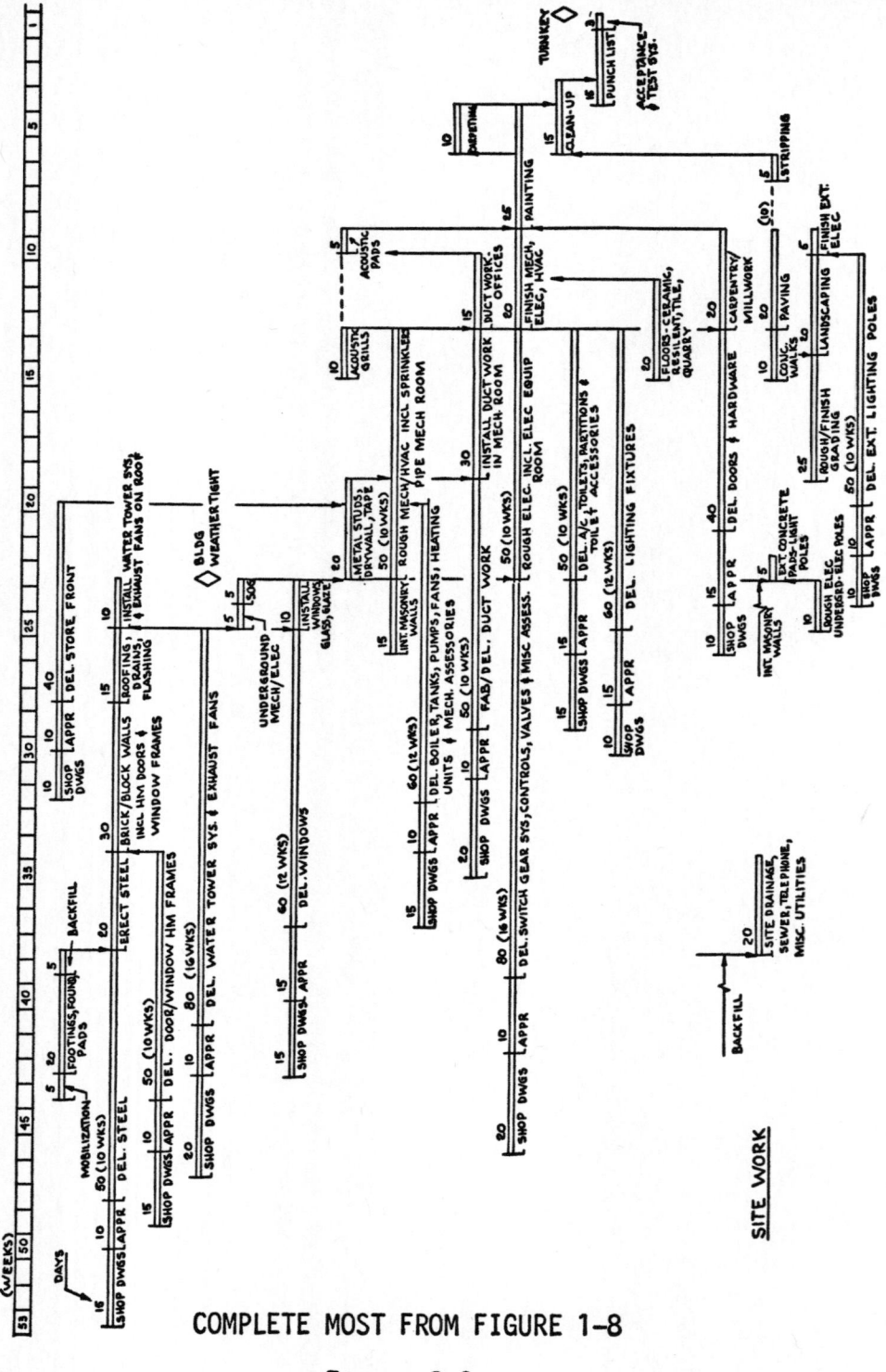

COMPLETE MOST FROM FIGURE 1-8

Figure 2-8

THE MOST ACTION PROGRAM FOR PROJECT CONTROL   67

THE MINI-MOST FOR A SHARPER FOCUS

Once the Baseline Schedule is distributed to everyone concerned, some of the subcontractors may not only want the total picture, but may also request a MOST schedule for their jobs only on a separate sheet of paper. They realize that they can more easily monitor their jobs if provided a separate MOST schedule focused on their activities. Their interrelationships and interfaces with other jobs will appear on the Baseline Schedule. These individual schedules are referred to as Mini-MOST.

Many of the subcontractors post the Mini-MOST in their site trailers alongside of the complete MOST. Some will take their updated Mini-MOST to project meetings to facilitate their review and coordination.

It is important to realize that if a Mini-MOST is distributed, it must be made very clear that it is a <u>supplementary</u> document to be used in conjunction with the complete schedule. Don't fall into the trap of allowing your subcontractors to proceed through the project while ignoring the constraints and interrelationships imposed on them by the other trades. If they are not in possession of the complete updated schedule, it will be too easy for them to say "I wasn't aware...."

To continue, we'll refer back to figure 2-8 and begin to create a Mini-MOST by separating all the jobs for the mechanical subcontractor. These jobs are:

> Drainage
> Sewage
> Mechanical Underground
> Rough Plumbing, including sprinklers
> Rough HVAC included in the mechanical room
> Deliver Boiler, Oil Tank
> Deliver Pumps, Fans
> Deliver Mechanical Accessories
> Deliver Air Conditioners
> Deliver Water Tower
> Deliver Heating Units
> Deliver Miscellaneous Mechanical Equipment
> Deliver Duct Work
> Prepare and Pipe Mechanical Room
> Deliver Toilets, Partitions, and Toilet Accessories
> Finish Plumbing
> Punch List Activities
> Run System
> Acceptance Test

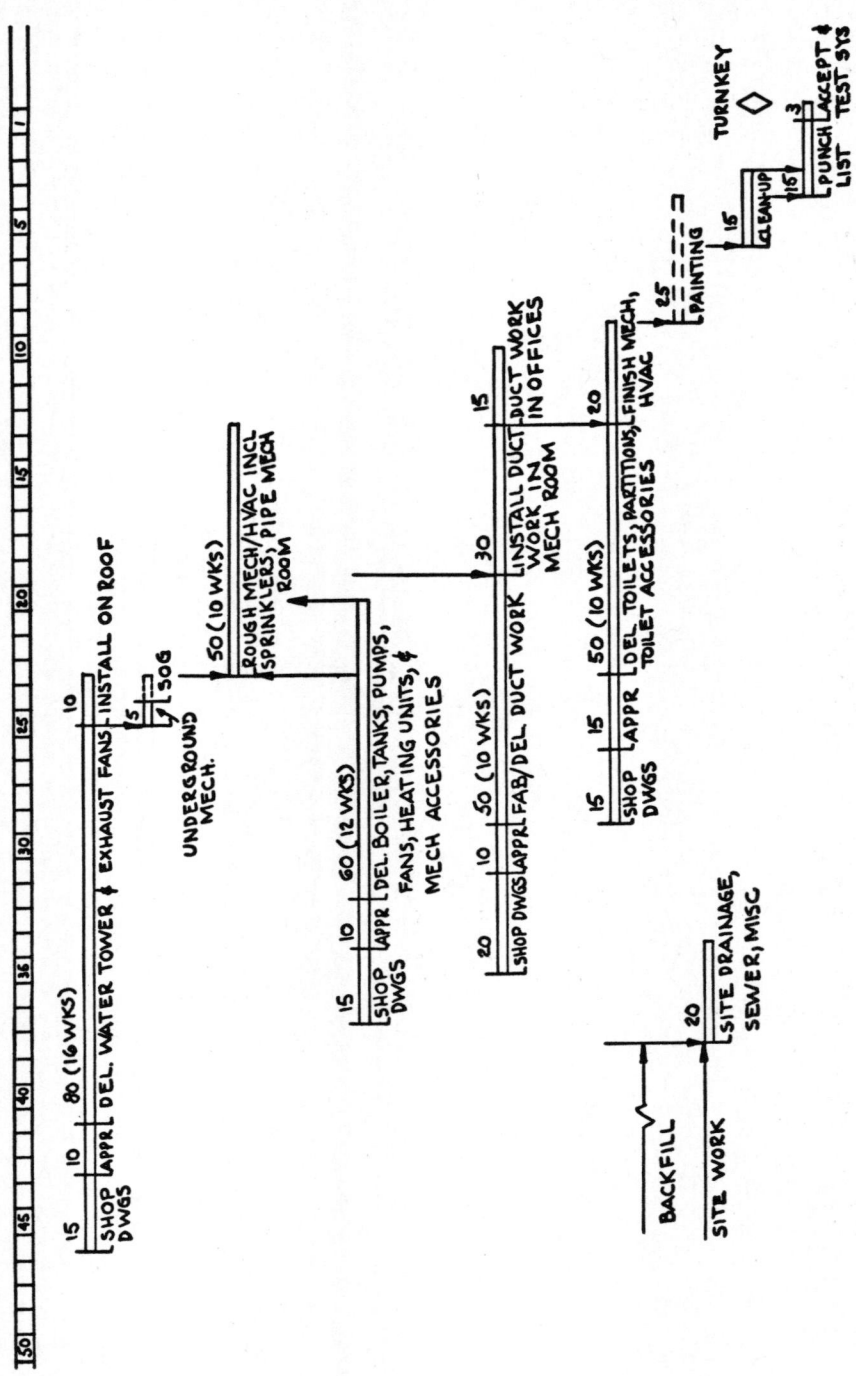

MINI-MOST (MECHANICAL SUBCONTRACTOR)

Figure 2-9

Figure 2-9 illustrates the Mini-MOST of these jobs using the same calendar dates for each item as they appear on the Baseline Schedule. It must be noted that when schedule work-around or get-well plans are made to either schedule, the changes must be included on both the Mini-MOST and the Baseline Schedules, with appropriate descriptions appearing in the Baseline Schedule Delay Notes. Communication and cooperation by both subcontractors and construction management are absolutely necessary to complete on schedule with a minimum of problems and interruptions.

BAR CHART LIMITATIONS

For years, many construction and building companies have relied on Bar Charts or Gantt Charts for their planning and scheduling needs, and will continue to do so if no other techniques are available to them. They have worked with many superintendents during the past and have become comfortable with bar charts because they can be close to reality and within schedule time (usually as a direct result of the competence of the site superintendent). These superintendents know within very close parameters when their construction projects will be completed. The problems that arise with these bar charts are that they are seldom updated or corrected, and cannot show where change orders are incorporated. Very few of these bar charts are submitted in litigation, mainly because history has not been retained, rescheduling does not appear with correct visibility, and the proper interdependencies and interrelationships of jobs are not generally apparent.

On the other extreme, when CPM is used for monitoring a project, many superintendents find CPM too cumbersome to use, or will simply not find the time to master its use. Some will retain their bar charts and transfer their inputs to the user of the CPM schedule. CPM is being used on many projects with success and will continue to be very successful. The majority of the largest firms in the country use CPM because it works for them. For those large companies that have been introduced to MOST, they elected to try MOST on a project or two while continuing CPM on the balance of their projects. After a short while, these companies realized the dynamic and economical value in the use of MOST and have decided to adopt MOST across the board. They now use CPM on very few occasions or on a limited basis.

Figure 2-10 illustrates a typical superintendent bar chart constructed from Figure 2-8. The inputs that are peculiar to MOST can never be realized on these bar charts. Because of their similarity in format, the transition to MOST for site personnel has never been difficult. Both systems are, you might say, bar charts.

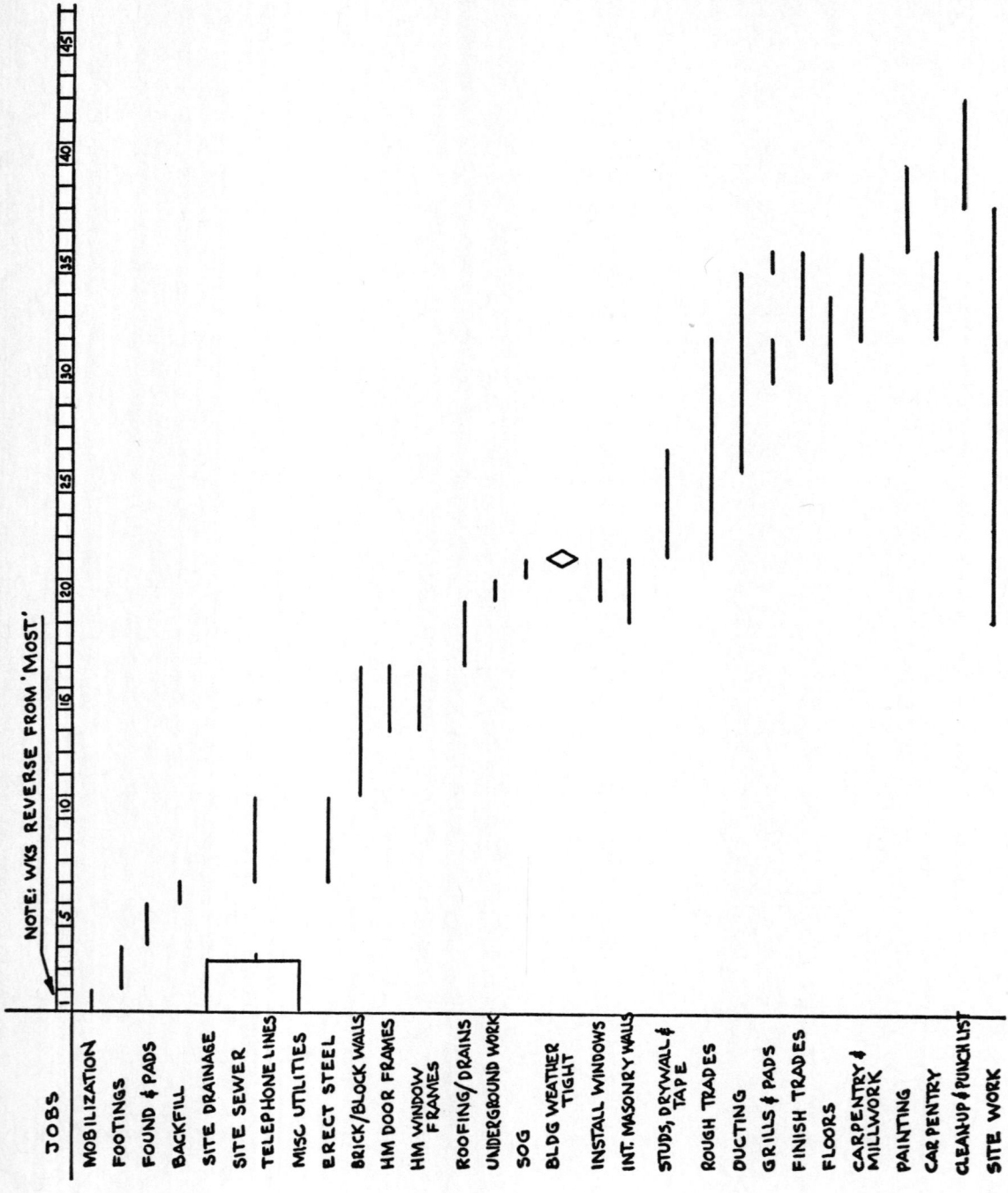

SAMPLE SUPERINTENDENT BAR CHART

Figure 2-10

THE MOST ACTION PROGRAM FOR PROJECT CONTROL

MOST, however, is probably the only technique that is referred to as a scheduling system due to the many different scheduling inputs and outputs that appear on a sheet of paper (more on this later).

KEEPING CHANGE ORDERS UNDER CONTROL

A Normal Part Of The Construction Process

Change orders in the construction business never end. They are usually changes above and beyond the initial designs of the project or recommended changes that increase or decrease the scope of the initial contract. In many cases, these changes are initiated by the architect and the owner and are issued by them. Regardless of who recommends them, insists upon them, or issues them, they are the household words in the construction business. If a scheduling technique cannot accommodate changes and their impacts, then it is easy to see how its use becomes marginal. Many construction schedulers have found it very difficult to include these change orders on their schedules and to correctly realize the schedule impact. Developing a get-well plan to overcome the effects of these change orders requires additional work. At times, it is not uncommon to have over 50 change orders on a project, with another 50 unapproved items of "claim" or backcharge potential. All these

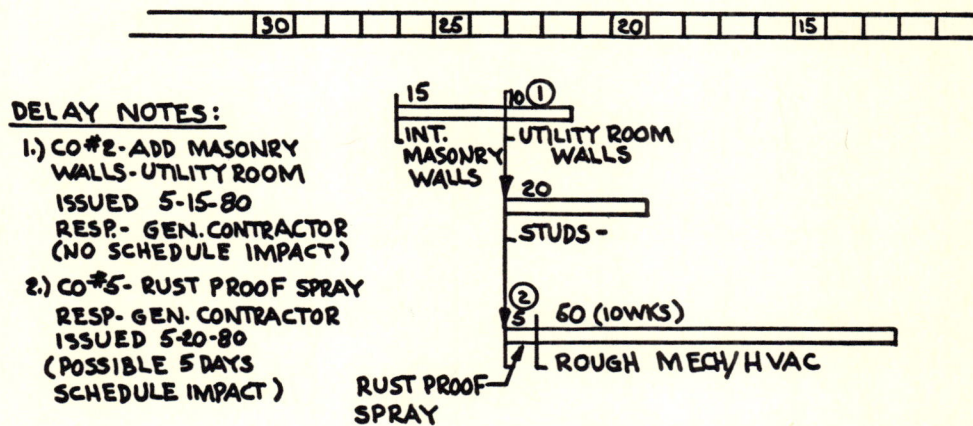

CHANGE ORDER SCHEDULE

Figure 2-11

changes are documented, dated, and negotiated, but, most often, they are not graphically illustrated in time, do not designate performance personnel, or do not totally describe the schedule impact that may occur. As a result, many dollars are lost for items that would have been legitimately part of the change order price.

The MOST system will conveniently and visibly display these change orders as they occur, and will show what effect they will have on the schedule, when they were received, whose responsibility it is to implement them, and the new completion date, if impact occurs. These change orders will be listed separately on the MOST schedule, in chronological order, and will be included in the schedule.

A look at Figure 2-11 will point out how to handle the change orders as mentioned in the previous paragraph. Note that these change orders should also be included in the Delay Notes column in their own entries as the explanation for the respective delays on affected activities. When posting these on the MOST schedule, the issue dates should be included. The change should be clearly noted, and all significant dates should be displayed. Many project managers, when following the above procedure, have found this to be a very powerful tool to account for and to schedule change orders. Project people at all levels have acknowledged that this technique has alleviated the worrisome handling of scheduling and accountability of change orders. Again, the ultimate goal is to give the immediate visibility of the impact of these change orders.

Schedule Impact

The absolute financial objectives of pricing and negotiating the change order, and the reasons why change orders exist are not within the purpose of this book. Of primary concern here is the timetable for these events, as well as the interaction of all parties affected by any contract modification, their organizations' interdependencies, accountabilities, and mutual responsibilities. The discussion below will treat the change order process and procedure from the beginning (recognition stage) to final resolution (payment). As in most business situations, each case in reality must be reviewed and acted upon for its own merits, but the lion's share will fit this example.

Many well-written construction contracts recognize that change orders, however large or small, interrupt planned operations and interfere with scheduled progress. They further recognize that this disruption may cause loss of efficiency, acceleration, material obsolescence, and additional materials and labor, but in any case will acknowledge the distinct probability that the price will increase. The last concept that good contracts recognize is that in all change order situations, timely action is required by everyone, including bureaucratic agencies, if the effects described above are to be minimized. Time is of the essence. It is for this reason that many contract specifications outline specific procedures to be followed by everyone in order to achieve the effective expediting of the paperwork. The often unfortunate circumstance, in spite of this foresight, is that many of the administrative personnel in an agency may not have a clear understanding of the need for prompt action, and the procedures may endure for the sake of the procedures themselves. The real objective of timely response may then become subordinated. The larger and more bureaucratic the organization or government agency, the more likely the possibility that this stagnation may occur at some level.

For this reason and for the reason that many contracts lack any provision for change order treatment, clear, accurate records must be kept of the entire change order progression — not only to support costs, negotiations, and claims — but to provide management and the project staff with the mechanism for tracking the status of the change, and expediting the respective phases directly with the appropriate people. It is necessary to begin this tracking before potential delays develop, thereby avoiding the constant firefighting which, too often, has become characteristic of contract modifications.

As discussed in detail in the section on MOST Financial Planning, two fundamental categories exist with respect to change orders:

> Type 1. Modifications which are not dependent upon previous contract activities, don't affect subsequent activities, and are thus wholly independent.

> Type 2. Modifications which are directly or indirectly related to and affected by previous and subsequent activities.

In practical application, the second type is most common in construction. The schedule impact of the first type should not, however, be understated, nor should its records be less thorough, primarily because inattention, inappropriate action, or lack of proper response by any of several parties early on may have a way of shifting the Type 1 change order to Type 2. Documentation of those events is essential.

Process and Procedure

Step 1. Identification/Notification

The first phase of any contract modification is the realization that a change order is warranted. This, most simply, is the determination and acknowledgement that work is required or desired that is not presently included in the contract. The legal descriptions of scopes of responsibility, errors and omissions, professional liability, design intent, and so on will not be explored here. What is needed for our analysis is simply the acknowledgement that a change to the contract is, indeed, appropriate.

It is at this stage that the notification time requirements of the contract and/or statute usually begin. Therefore, it is one of the most important areas of the change order documentation. Depending upon the individual circumstances, this identification may be made by the general contractor's field or administrative personnel, subcontractors, suppliers, the owner, the architect, or the engineer. In any case, the owner must be immediately formally notified, the issue defined, and acknowledgement of the change order requirement secured. This is very often the most difficult and time-consuming part of all administrative phases of a contract modification. It therefore behooves the contractor to record the event on the construction schedule to begin to illustrate all subsequent impacts.

At this point, then, indicate on the current revision the activities affected, and reference all appropriate correspondence, as in Figure 2-12.

Note the definite activity duration assigned (5 days in the example) for the owner, architect, and engineer to get together, finalize the design, and issue a scope of work, complete with all appropriate material specifications, plans, and details that will allow the change order to be priced. At the moment the change order is acknowledged to be legitimate, commitment by the owner and the designers must be confirmed, and a definitive timetable set for the issuance of the necessary information. It is this committment that is the first item posted on the schedule. In this way, accountability for all change order phases is established at the start. As a footnote, it will also be helpful to secure from the owner his or her estimate of the time required for review of the forthcoming change order proposal (10 days in Figure 2-13). This information will be used in the next phase, and its legitimacy will have been maintained.

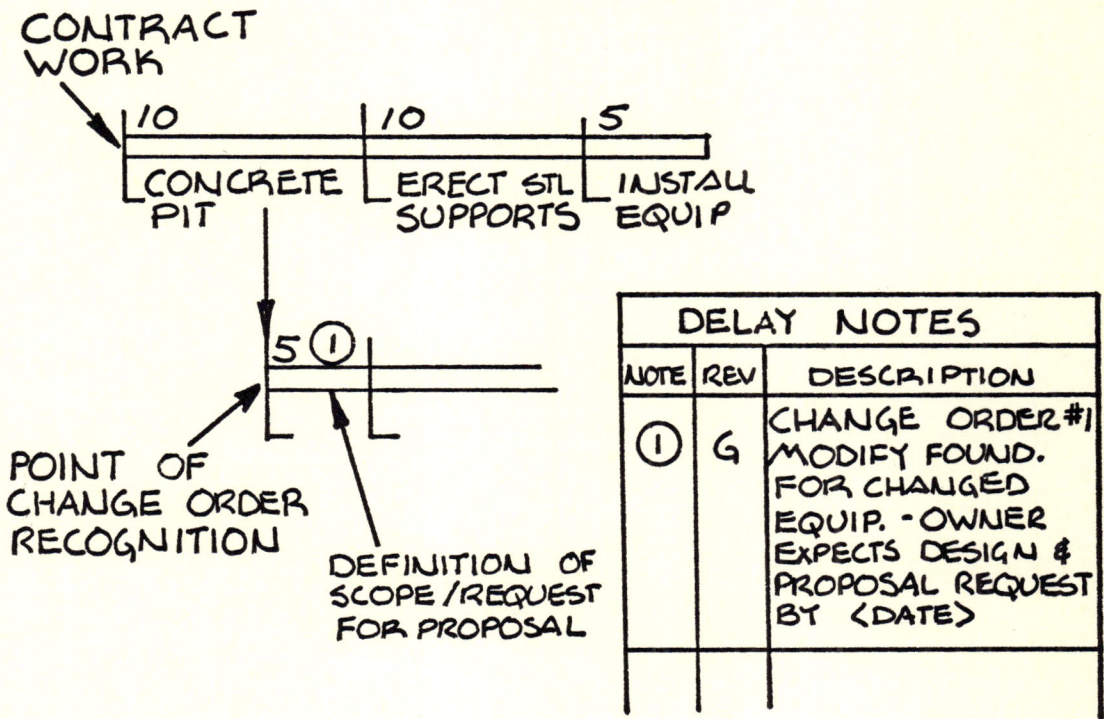

NOTIFICATION OF CHANGE ORDER

Figure 2-12

Step 2. Determine Schedule Impact

Immediately upon receipt of the change order design and description, schedule the work in detail and determine the total impact on the project. It is important to complete this phase now, because it is precisely this detailed information that will be needed to be sure that the change order proposal is thorough, professional, and considers all compensable variables. Care must be taken to insure that activity durations are included for all preparatory items (see Figure 2-13).

The value of completing this process <u>before</u> the proposal is constructed should be evident. Just for starters, suppose that this "quick" 5-day change is really going to take 42 days to consummate; the actual delay is significantly greater than what might have been assumed. This is really a common situation. It is not difficult to see how change orders involving several trades, critical

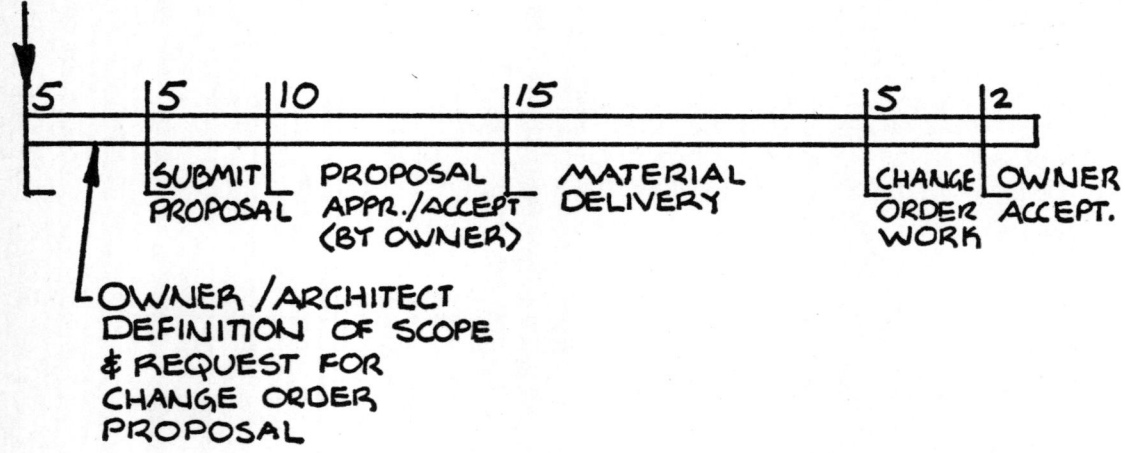

CHANGE ORDER LEAD TIMES

Figure 2-13

sequencing, long material delivery lead times, and many other variables can quickly impact construction work in ways greatly out of proportion to the actual cost of the changed work. That extra $150 piece of security hardware may take a year to get, and interfere with subsequent work. For this reason, intense scrutiny and attention to detail is absolutely necessary.

Another example of the tenacity of this effect might be in the type of ploy sometimes attempted by unscrupulous owners which, at best, delays contract payments and, at worst, results in a claim.

For background: many construction contracts contain provisions which maintain the owner's right to direct the contractor to include change order work that is "within the scope of the contract." The vagueness of this description is the heart of the problem. When a project is somewhere between 90% and 98% complete, and the contractor is looking forward to the imminent project closeout and release of retainage (a percentage of all contract payments that has been held back by the owner as a kind of security for faithful performance) there are suddenly a few (or a flood of) requests for change order proposals for items which are small in dollar value and which may or may not be required to complete the project as a whole. They may either, of course, be Type 1 or Type 2 change orders as discussed earlier. The interesting effect is that when these modifications to the contract are scheduled, they most often have a way of projecting themselves way off into the future—weeks beyond the current completion date.

The first significant effect is that the contractor(s) must remain mobilized on the site for the period, and the project overhead might continue at nearly the same rate as during the more intensive phases of construction - way out of proportion to the small amount of new work. Temporary facilities, administrative functions, superintendence, and so on must be maintained. The more serious condition, though, is that the retainage amount due the contractor will be held by the owner throughout that period. To illustrate the significance: 5% retainage on a $3 million contract that is 100% complete is $150,000 payment due. This entire payment could, for example, be delayed the entire six weeks that it takes you to finish that "$2000" change order.

All of these things may not be completely adverse conditions within and among themselves, but the important thing is that you be aware of their existence to allow for their consideration in the treatment of the change order. One option may be to include these effects as part of the change order price (intensive overhead, carrying charges for the retainage, etc.). The problem in this case, however, is that these costs will usually greatly outweigh the actual cost of the additional work, may not be recognized by the owner in their legitimate amounts, and a claim might arise. Another distinct possibility is for the additional work to be refused to be performed because of the grossly disproportionate costs, which places the proposed contract modification out of the realm of the "scope" of the contract. Review the contract documents and secure legal advice in this regard before proceeding. Having all these disproportionate effects clearly displayed on the schedule in an easily understood format will backup your explanations and strongly substantiate your position.

In these and similar situations, the MOST schedule will, in the final analysis, be the clear documentation that will quantify the specific details of any related claim.

Step 3. Solicit Subcontractor Change Order Proposals

Upon management's decision to move ahead in the process, proposals must be solicited from all subcontractors affected. Every subcontractor, even the most remotely involved, must be notified of the pending change to allow them the opportunity to review the effects. This is simply good business practice. If the changed work does not effect the subcontractor, it is most helpful to have that fact secured in writing from the respective party. This will prevent many unpleasant repercussions downstream, and preclude the possibility of omissions on the part of the general contractor.

Exhibit 1 is a word-for-word form letter which may be used to solicit the change order information from the various subcontractors. The underlying objective is to secure quickly and completely information regarding all possible effects of the change. What the subcontractor is striving for in the items listed for consideration is that:

1. All cost factors be included, including any applicable credits; the proposal is to be complete the first time.

2. The proposal, including all cost breakdowns, is constructed in conformance with any conditions contained in the specifications - in the proper format.

3. All schedule information, including delivery and erection times, interdependencies, etc. is confirmed to either support or correct the schedule as constructed in Step 2.

4. 1, 2, and 3 above are accomplished in a timely manner to allow the acceptable submission of the general proposal to the owner. This is the important reason for the stronger language at the letter's closing. Urgency must be stressed.

It will also be helpful to call each recipient of the letter first, to set the process in motion as quickly as possible. The letter, then, will simply become a confirming document.

THE MOST ACTION PROGRAM FOR PROJECT CONTROL

EXHIBIT 1

Letter to Subcontractors Requesting Change Order Proposal

Re: (Project Identification)

Subject: (Request for Change Order Proposal Description)

Subcontractor #1
Subcontractor #2
Subcontractor #3

Gentlemen:

Attached is the (insert owner name and date) Request for Change Order Proposal regarding the subject.

If the work included herein does not affect your work, please submit your confirmation of no change in the contract price.

If the changed work does involve your company, please immediately submit:

* Price to perform the changed work.
* Any applicable credit for eliminated contract work.
* Substantiating breakdowns.
* Material/equipment delivery times after change order approval.
* Time required to perform the work (separate major items).
* Work of any other trade affected.
* Any special conditions necessary to perform the work.
* Any significant weather, site, or other constraints beyond your control.
* All other applicable information.

Your complete response is required by (date) in order to allow the timely submission of the general proposal.

Your action beyond that date may cause excessive delays in the work; all costs for which must be backcharged.

Thank you for your cooperation.

                                  Closing

cc: Superintendent

Step 4. Submit The General Proposal To The Owner

The specifications must be reviewed to be sure that all applicable contractual obligations are included (percentages of overhead and profit, quantity calculations, unit prices, and so on). After the price is substantiated, all other significant considerations must be highlighted. These might include:

1. All direct costs, including supervision and superintendence.

2. Time extensions.

3. Date of required proposal acceptance by owner (Show that absolute interference will occur by this date, causing cost increases which will then be submitted for payment).

4. Note that the proposal is for work expressly described only; additional effects caused by subsequent changes must be charged.

5. Reservation of all rights to claim damages related to the extension of time.

Step 5. Document

Include in the delay notes the impact on all activities affected. From this point on, this work and all parties will be coordinated, expedited, followed upon and recorded as were all items in the original contract. You can move in the direction of the project completion with confidence in the realization that you've thoroughly taken care of the cause, and while the effects won't necessarily take care of themselves, they will have been well provided for.

MULTIPROJECT SCHEDULING FOR TOTAL CONTROL

When a construction company has more than one construction project underway at a given time, its management would like to know the status of each and how each is progressing relative to each other. The first reason for this is to allow management to program priorities and relocate resources if needed. Management wants a warm feeling that all projects are under schedule and project management control. Management wants to "level" the work load among its project managers in order to have a smoother operation to realize its profits and satisfy its customers. Of at least equal importance, this information is required to a reliable degree to satisfy bonding and insurance requirements, as well as banks (credit lines, etc.).

There are many ways to illustrate what has come to be known as Multiproject Scheduling, but displaying the multiproject stack-up as in Figure 2-14 significantly improves visibility and understanding for project and upper management. With this visibility, the number of site superintendents are known as well as when they are dropped off, when they can be available for their next project, how many project managers are used, and when they will be available to manage another project. Of particular importance to upper management is the timing of the percentages or completions of the various projects. From experience, we have found this technique to be extremely valuable and easy to use for downstream planning, because many large construction companies today do not formally prepare for long-range planning.

Assuming that a MOST schedule has been prepared and is being monitored for each project, the updated status from each detailed MOST can be posted on a Multiproject Scheduling Form (see Figure 2-15). At the updating line in the example, June 30 projects 9, 10, and 11 have been projected but not started. Project 8 is late starting. These eleven projects are on the books, and when others are awarded, they will be added and programmed for project managers and site superintendent selections. It should be construction management's responsibility to see that this multiproject schedule form is updated as often as possible for the best decision making in the profit interest of the company.

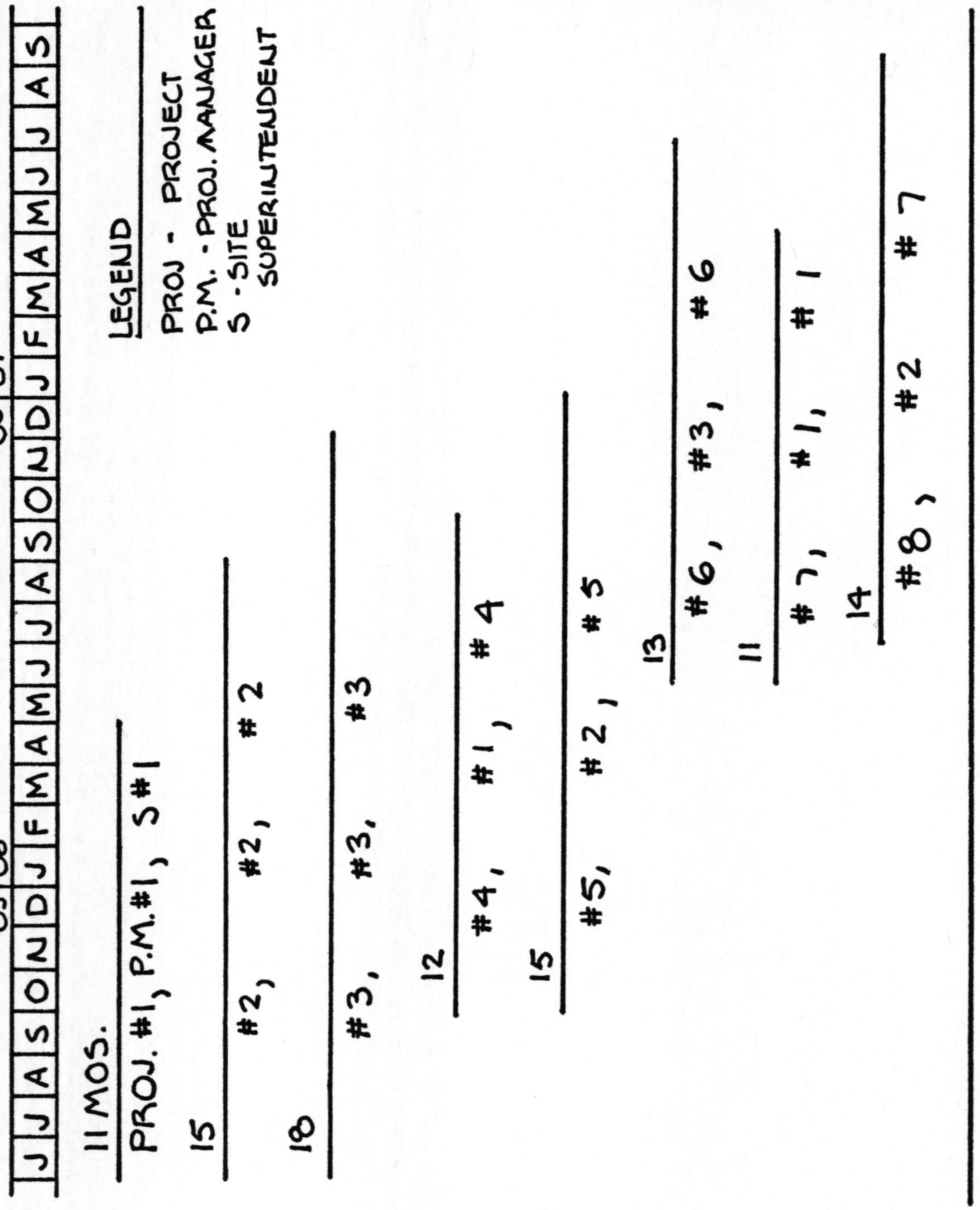

MULTIPROJECT SCHEDULE

Figure 2-14

85/86	86/87
J J A S O N D J F M A M J J A S O N D	J F M A M J J A S

11 MOS. PROJ. #1, P.M.#1, S#1

15 — #2, #2, #2

18 — #3, #3, #3

12 — #4, #1, #4

15 — #5, #2, #5

13 — #6, #3, #6

11 — #7, #1, #1

14 — #8, #2, #7

LEGEND
PROJ - PROJECT
P.M. - PROJ. MANAGER
S - SITE SUPERINTENDENT

THE MOST ACTION PROGRAM FOR PROJECT CONTROL 83

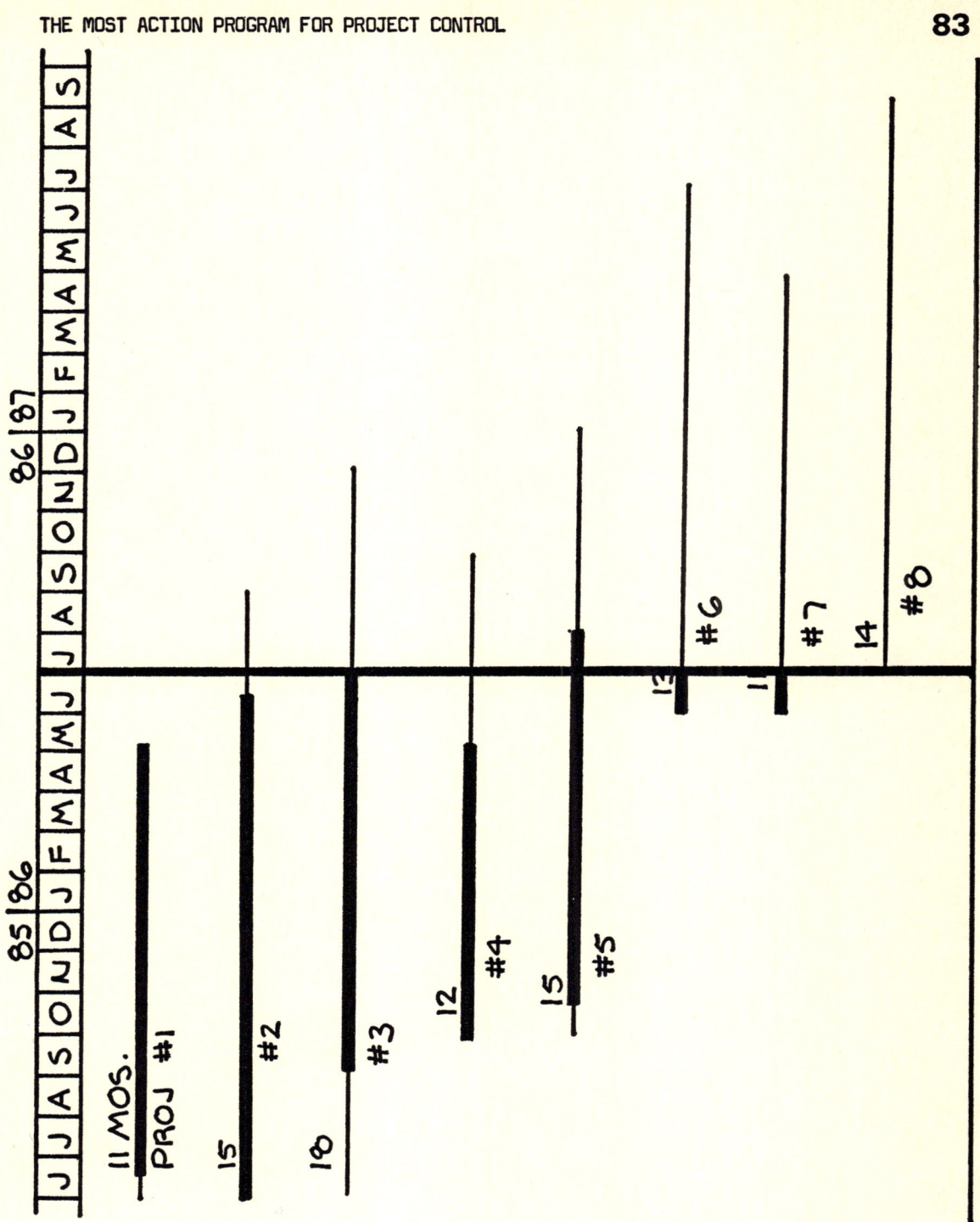

UPDATED MULTIPROJECT SCHEDULE

Figure 2-15

A quick review of the multiproject form will reveal that it is, of course, nothing more than a schedule summarizing the project output of the entire organization. As such, reviewing any current revision will provide answers to questions such as:

* What is my forecasted total production for (any point in time)?

* How does that forecasted production compare with the known company production capacity? (Very helpful when dealing with bonding people.) Do I need to step up marketing, or increase capacity?

* Are administrative overhead and project people with specific skills being distributed most efficiently?

* Are certain administrative and supervisory personnel being over- or under-worked?

* How are progress payments timed; will delaying or accelerating downstream projects improve desired cash flow?

* How will forecasted percentages of total capacity (at various points in time) affect bidding and negotiating strategies and objectives - do we need work, or can we afford to hold out for jobs with better profitability?

It soon becomes obvious that the more the multiproject form is contemplated, the more numerous and diverse applications become evident. Be creative; explore how this simple but powerful analysis can best suit your company.

THE COUNTDOWN SCHEDULE FOR SYSTEMATIC COMPLETION

Generally, when there are about two months remaining on a project and the master schedule is marked up with many last minute changes, the project manager may wish to prepare a final schedule showing all the miscellaneous jobs to be completed. This is called the Countdown Schedule. This schedule will be prepared in days and monitored in days. In this way, all of the minor jobs that would not be included in the master schedule can be shown together with jobs that have been postponed or not completed with two months remaining.

Many of the cleanup jobs and punch list jobs can now be illustrated. Also, many of the trades' miscellaneous jobs that did not appear on earlier schedules now need day-to-day attention. Figure 2-16 illustrates a typical Countdown Schedule.

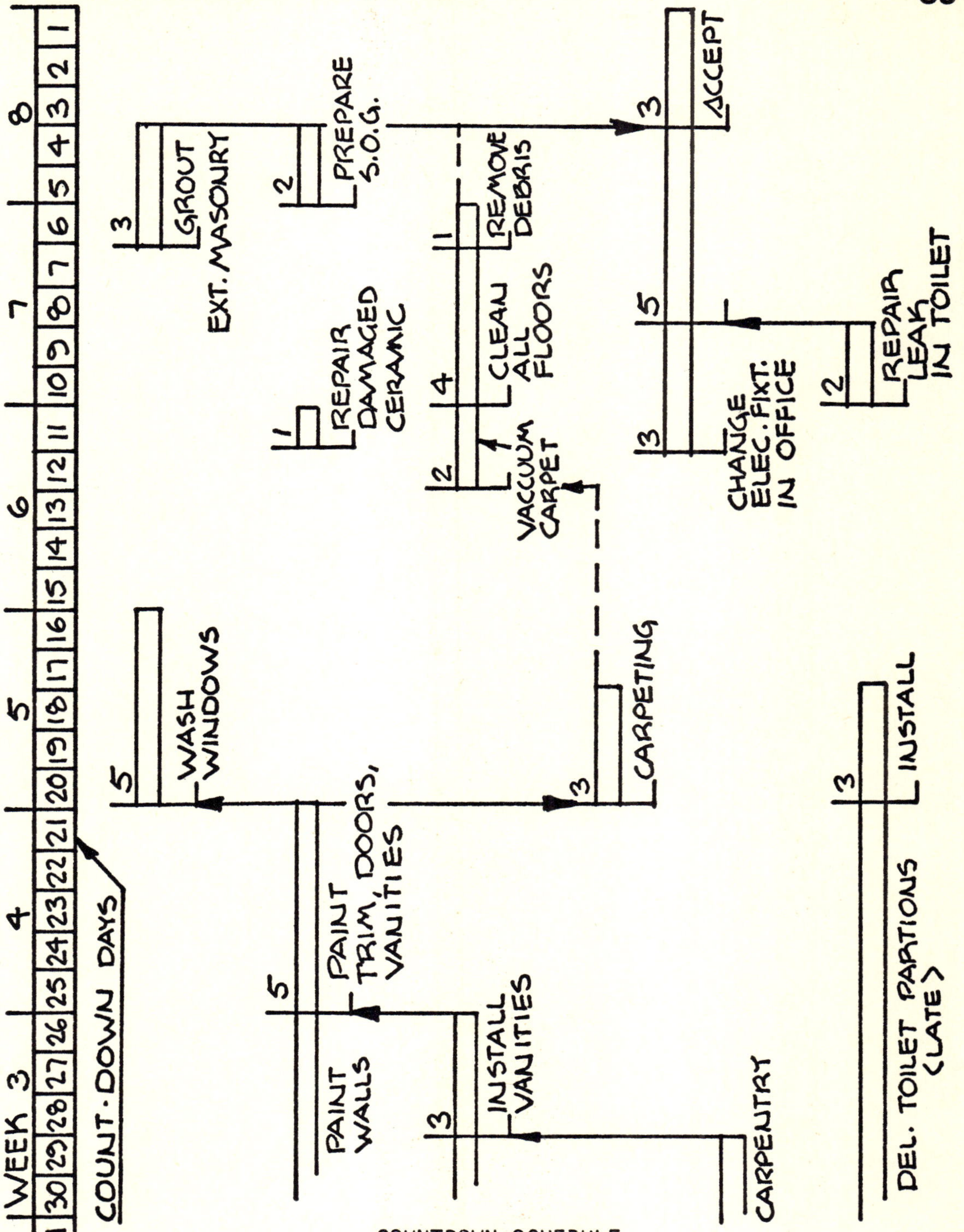

THE MOST ACTION PROGRAM FOR PROJECT CONTROL 85

COUNTDOWN SCHEDULE

Figure 2-16

No matter how competent the scheduling team may be, the changing nature of construction schedules makes it impossible to anticipate field conditions and all effects precipitated by contract modifications, reschedules, etc. that will occur near the final phases of nearly every project. For this reason, it is important to recognize that the probability of corrections, improvements, or simply the desire for greater level of detail is high.

The Countdown Schedule is <u>not</u> a replacement or substitute for the master project schedule at this point, but rather (just as with a Mini-MOST), it is a supplement.

The inclusion of these fine-tuned items and their tracking on a day-to-day basis make their coordinated completion rapid and efficient. Updates of the Countdown Schedule will reflect the status relative to the Countdown Schedule itself, but project management must not lose sight of the perspective of the Countdown Schedule relative to those activities' (and their parts) status on the master schedule current revision. For example, the activities "Paint Walls" and "Paint Trim, Doors, and Vanities" may be on or ahead of schedule in the Countdown update, but in reality they, as well as other parts of the Countdown may be months late relative to the original schedule because of some previous delay (possibly late window deliveries).

Your updates, then, would show an acceptable progress on the Countdown Schedule, but overall project status would still be indicated on the master schedule.

This same concept applies equally to all seperate detailed "get-well" plans that may have been issued during the life of the project.

3
Winning in Court and Arbitration with MOST

The information that is retained on the MOST construction schedule, such as delay notes, that include change orders, down time, inclement weather, or acts of God, will be useful for the legal department in preparing the brief as to why the problem occurred and who is responsible. Naturally, the cause for rescheduling and extending the schedule will be evident on the MOST schedule. It is therefore important to retain all revisions. The superintendent's daily logs and the entire project record should support the schedules.

CLAIMS-CONSCIOUSNESS IN CONSTRUCTION SCHEDULING

The primary objective of any construction schedule is to complete the project as designed in a systematic, coordinated manner, and in the shortest time consistent with cost and manpower constraints, thereby maintaining a good profit. The construction process, however, does not occur in a vacuum. Contingencies must be provided for, and the realization must be acknowledged that many differences exist among the large spectrum of organizations and individuals that will be involved to varying degrees during the life of the project. The construction schedule should not be prepared with the philosophy that claims will be a definite result and will therefore be maximized, but rather, it should be "claims conscious;" constructed and updated in a clear, consistent manner with complete, thorough notes and references that can easily be assembled, categorized, and supported in the event of a claim. A good construction schedule will easily provide significant, visible comparisons and convincing proof of damages, including delay, acceleration, suspension of work, inefficiencies, disruption, and interference.

The discussion that follows is not intended to be exhaustive with respect to the subject of all legal requirements and considerations, but the material will provide thorough, concise descriptions of the general ideas and philosophies that are the fundamental basis for good records, clear accountability, and effective presentation. The "claims conscious" manager may by his or her actions, head off more problems, thereby actually reducing the number of claims. But, more importantly, in the event of a claim, management can proceed with appropriate action with confidence rooted in the knowledge that a complete and thorough preparation has been effected.

The following illustrations are examples of some typical Mini-MOST schedules that will support the updated MOST schedules. These schedules can be included in the prepared legal briefs. Their visibility will show the slippages from planned jobs and what effect they had on the contractual completion date. If these slippages and illustrations are in your favor, it is wise to schedule-educate your legals in order that they have a full understanding of their contents. Your attorneys can only act in your behalf with understandable data. Superintendent bar charts may not stand up in court because they are generally not kept up to date or corrected to reflect true progress or true integrations and interrelationships.

Because of the many variables associated with scheduling problems in the construction business, only a few of the more common types confronted by many building companies will be illustrated. Figure 3-1 illustrates how inclement weather influences the schedule. Note that it is the planned date, that from the baseline schedule, which will be compared with the actual date of completion to reflect the negative variance.

Figure 3-2 is an example illustrating the effects of change orders on the planned work.

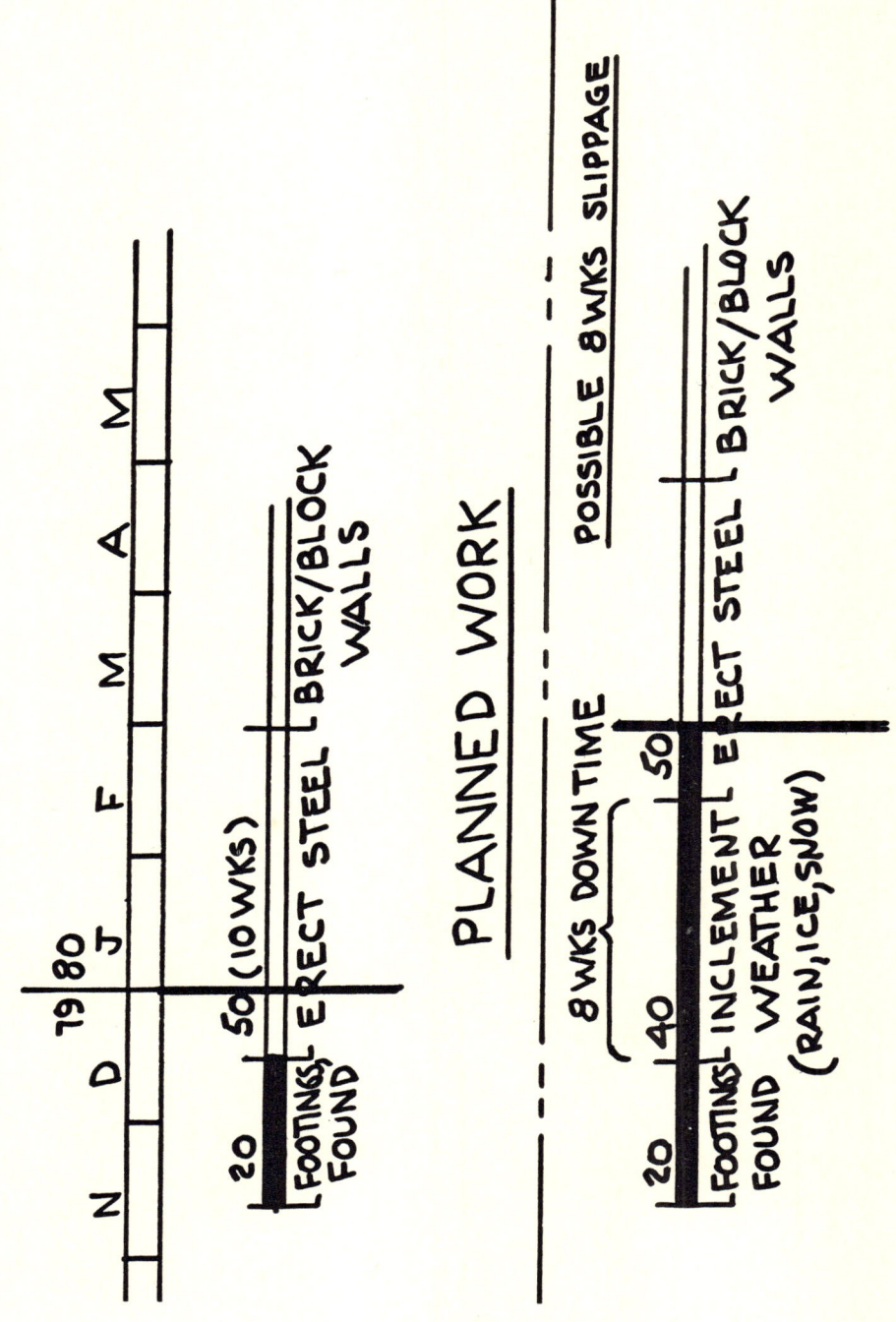

ACTUAL WORK PERFORMED

Figure 3-1

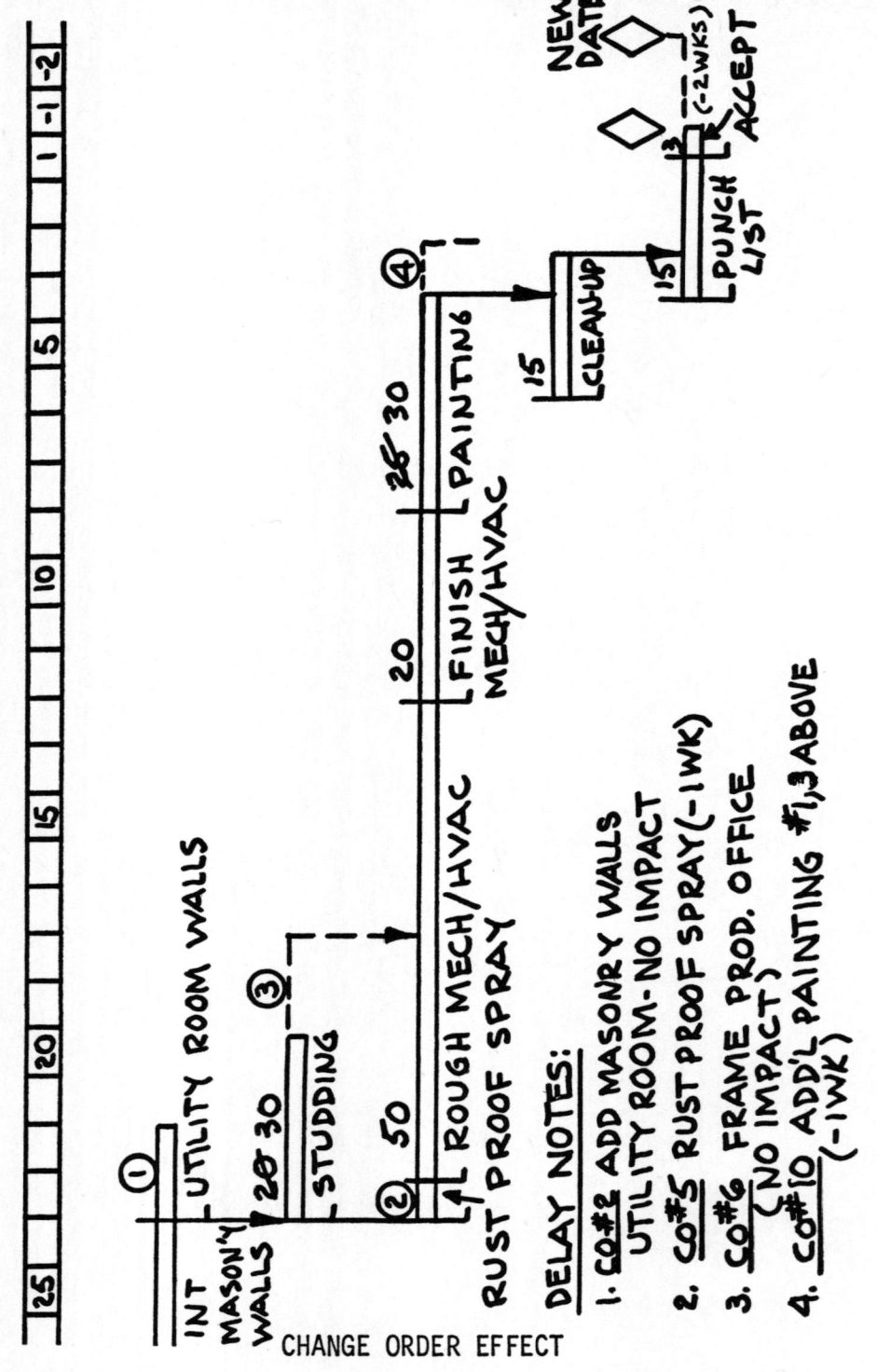

Figure 3-2

Figure 3-3 shows a common schedule sequence often used by general contractors. Not all reschedules may be caused by other parties, but the effects of all slippages must be shown.

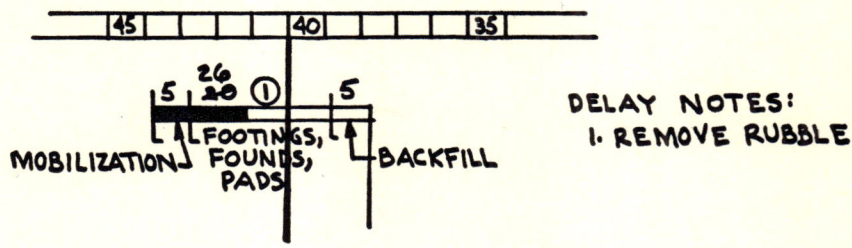

SLIPPAGES

Figure 3-3

A final consolidation of all the above effects is completed to illustrate the real total impact on the completion date. This is shown in Figure 3-4, below.

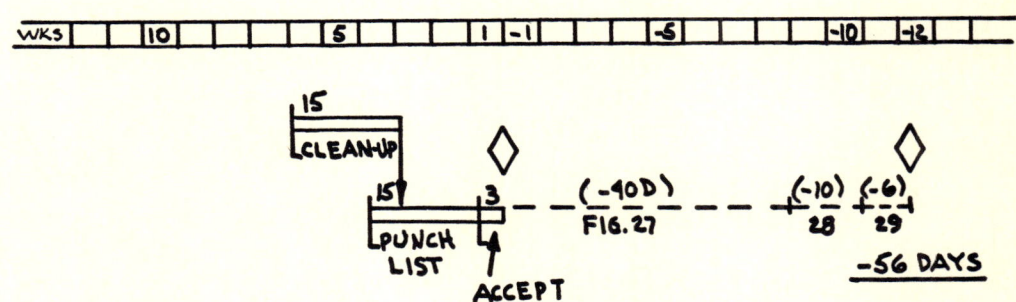

TOTAL SCHEDULE IMPACT

Figure 3-4

Figure 3-4.A on the following page illustrates how faulty waterproofing material coupled with snow, ice, and cold affected the

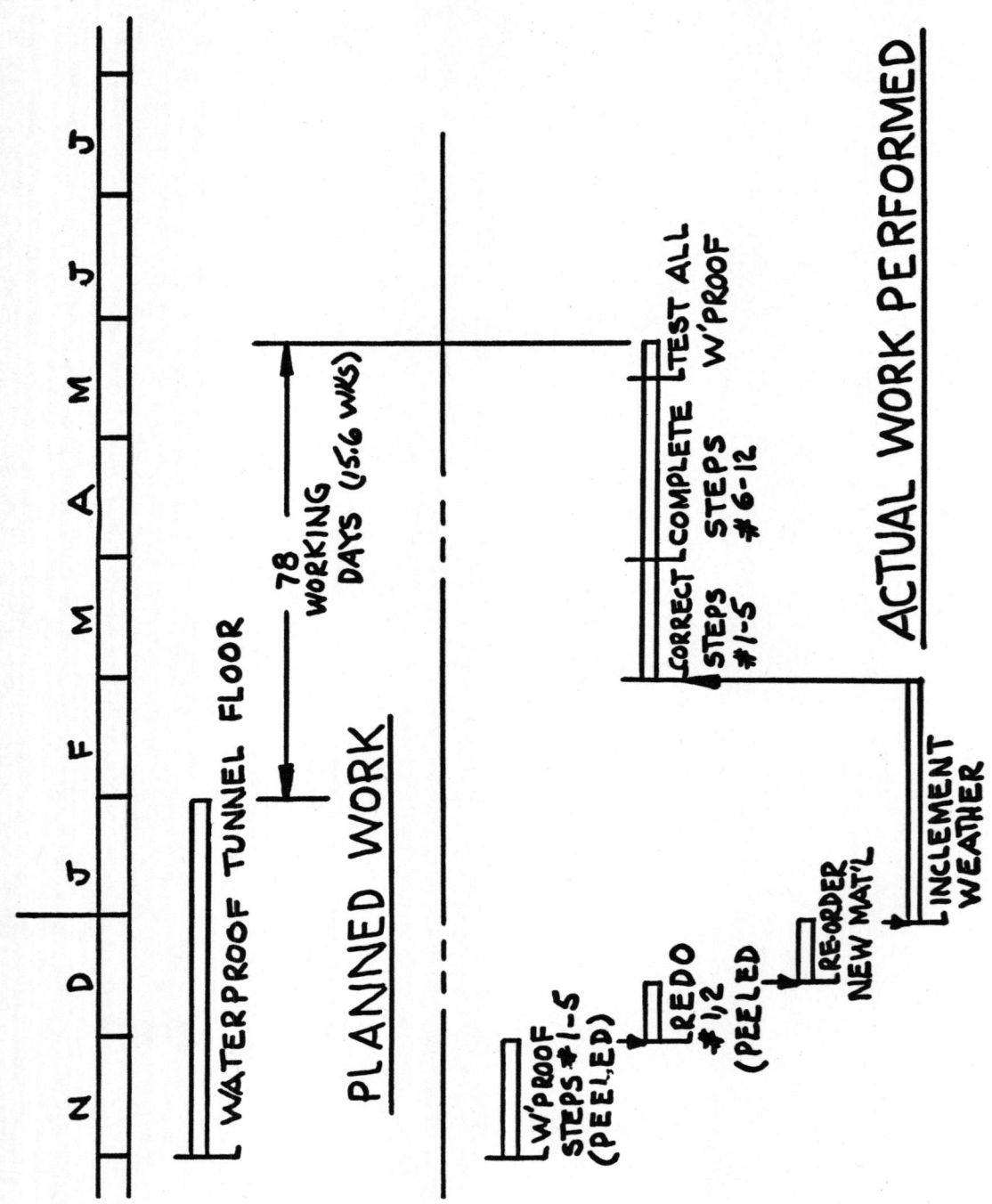

PLANNED vs ACTUAL WORK

Figure 3-4.A

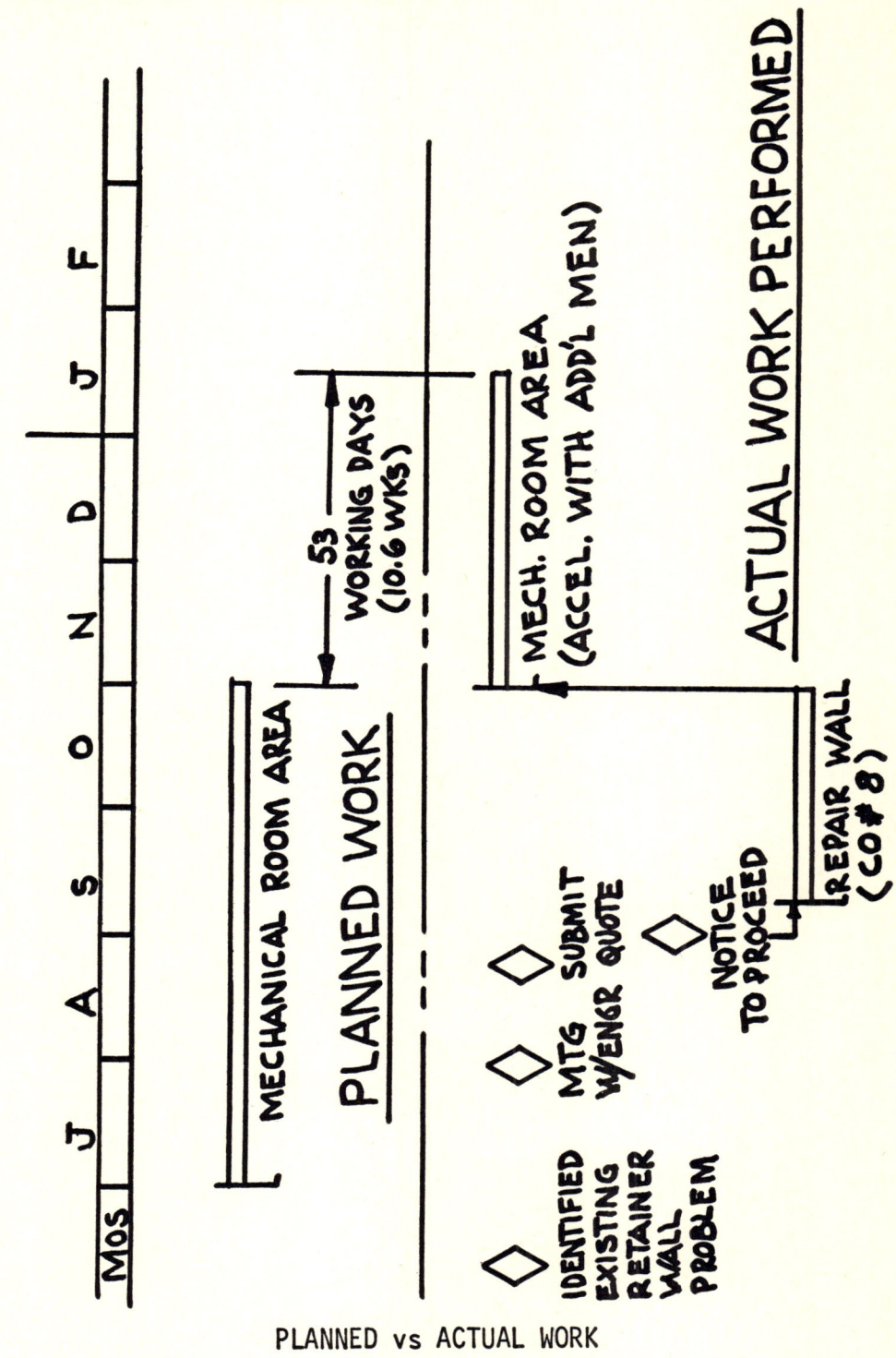

PLANNED vs ACTUAL WORK

Figure 3-4.B

planned schedule. These effects are not the responsibility of the general contractor, and the time lost (clearly quantified by MOST) should be compensated for. Figure 3-4.B is another example showing additional schedule problems that were overlooked. Again, these should be paid for by the party(ies) responsible; the general contractor cannot be expected to "absorb" it.

All of these Mini-MOST and final updated MOST schedules are excellent backup documents to be included in legal briefs and presentations. It is also helpful to include a short write-up for each schedule in the event any document has to stand alone.

Successful use of this approach has encouraged many construction firms to adopt the MOST system, even after the fact, to improve the presentation and understandability of CPM schedules that may have been used. Many lawyers involved have attested that using the clear MOST presentations has most certainly helped win their cases. Some have filed their winning cases under the name of "Construction with MOST."

SIX REQUIREMENTS FOR PRESENTABLE EVIDENCE

Several general criteria exist that are helpful to include, and/or may be required if a construction schedule will even be allowed to be presented in court. Even if the rules of evidence and judicial opinion are being considered in a less technical sense, as is possible in arbitration, the application of these ideas can only help substantiate the legitimacy of the schedule and its usefulness as a legal document. The descriptions that follow may not strictly fit technical legal requirements, but the general ideas are important. You are strongly advised to consult with legal professionals for more detailed opinions, but, in any case, the information that follows will prove to be most useful.

1. The schedule must be the one that was actually used to build the project. Even if a schedule that is substantially different from the one under consideration has been formally submitted previously, and approved by the owner and/or the design professionals, the schedule that was actually used and depended upon by the various trades will generally be considered to be the legitimate document.

2. The schedule must be periodically revised. It is generally recognized that construction scheduling, however an exact or inexact science it may be, is nothing more than a plan to construct what can reasonably be construed from the contract documents, notwithstanding the fact that there

may be several ways to build the same project. Although contingencies may be included to allow for indefinitely defined variables, there probably has never been a schedule constructed that anticipated every problem, coordinated every piece, and required no modifications. Changes to or correcting of the plan, then, is inevitable. The schedule, therefore, must be updated periodically to maintain a current and accurate representation of reality, if its presentation to any court or arbitration panel is to remain credible. The revisions must be founded on the project record.

3. The periodic updates must show all positive and negative influences by all parties; none must be singled out; none must be absent for convenience. If all updates, for example, only indicate delays caused by the owner and fail to delineate other known problems caused by other parties, it won't be be very difficult for your opponent to clearly demonstrate the bias that has been built into the document, and again, the legitimacy and credibility of the schedule in its entirety will begin to crumble. In other words, failure to recognize all significant events will bring into question the validity of the entire schedule presentation.

4. The schedule must include realistic construction logic and activity durations to demonstrate the professional ability of the scheduler. Illogical sequences or the lack of consideration of important variables (such as indicating the installation of a 25,000 gallon tank in a building with no overhead doors to occur before the roof is constructed) will only quickly demonstrate that the constraints in the schedule were unrealistic to begin with. The gravity of the commitments made by others to these constraints will become vague at best.

5. The schedule must fairly represent the actual method planned to build the project. If, for example, the schedule had been prepared primarily to cater to progress payments, or was otherwise unrelated to actual construction of the project, it will become very clear that as a tool for managing the project, its value will be marginal. Its use for proving the legitimacy of a claim will be correspondingly minimal.

6. The schedule updates and analysis must be realistic and in perspective. An overly aggressive computation of damages may damage the validity of the entire analysis. Direct cause/effect relationships must be shown.

In addition to the above, make sure that all notes and references are correlated with the more detailed chronological project correspondence, and have all field notes, claims, commitments, deadlines, and promises detailed in the Delay Notes. Also include the dates and the names of the people of the respective organizations supplying information. Pin it down.

Generally, three types of schedules may be used in a claim presentation. The "As Planned" Schedule is the MOST Baseline Schedule which shows how the contractor proposed to build the project. The "As Built" schedule is the updated MOST schedule that records how the work was actually performed and the time required to complete each activity. The "Adjusted" schedule is the MOST schedule that reconstructs the project to show how it would have been performed if the effects of the subject claim are removed. This is the most difficult and probably the most time consuming to prepare. In constructing the adjusted schedule, it is important to include all events and effects described in (3) on page 95.

If the managers and all project administrative personnel are cognizant of the ideas and the fundamental processes of a claim presentation, the records being kept and assembled by all will be more consistent and complete with respect to their ultimate use. It is this type of thoroughness and attention to detail that will ultimately bring about more consistent success in claims.

4
MOST as Timely Notice of Damages, Backcharges, and Claims

IMPROVEMENTS IN PERFORMANCE AND PROTECTION OF RIGHTS

To this point, we've seen what the MOST construction schedule is, how to construct it, updating techniques to report current status, treatments of modifications to the contract, the value of the document to easily consolidate clear, concise records, and some uses of the schedule to substantiate claims. All of this may significantly elevate the organizational level of professionalism with respect to planning, operating, directing, coordinating, and controlling the project. However, the ability of the MOST (or any other) schedule to legally and practically commit the various organizations and individuals to the timetables, sequences, and constraints, and, in general, bind everyone who might conceivably require it, is directly related to its distribution and notification in a timely manner.

In addition, right from the start you must realize that there exists the distinct possibility that any or several subcontractors or suppliers may treat this or any schedule with an attitude that is much too casual for effective project control. Production meetings may be attended with whatever level of consistency, dates may be confirmed, and commitments may be acknowledged, but for some reason that subcontractor or supplier may, in spite of all their "coordination" efforts, still manage to waltz through the life of the project with a hit-and-miss production schedule that no one is aware of. The frustrating thing about this is that there may really be no malicious intentions or conscious neglect involved. The offending parties may simply not realize or understand the implications of their lack of coordinated effort. This case most often occurs in contracts where the general contractor has minimal or no control over the selection of the particular subcontractor(s), as in the case of pre-filed sub bids or other direct owner preference. Also, the MOST technique for documenting the lack of or inappropriate performance as detailed in Chapter 3 will certainly substantiate claims against this party. Yet, the prudent contractor must realize that while all this protection might be comforting, it is not getting the job built correctly and on time.

The objectives of this chapter then, are to explore the concept of timely notice, delineate the procedure for posting and distributing the MOST schedule, develop the Schedule Analysis/ Evaluation Report, and outline several basic ideas which may help to improve the performance of problem subcontractors and suppliers before things get out of hand. As appropriate, word-for-word letters will be included for you to retype on your own letterhead and use during your own administration of the MOST construction schedule (refer to the important copyright notice at the front of this book).

REQUIREMENTS AND ADVANTAGES OF PROPER NOTICE

The original compilation of data and construction of the baseline schedule is completed in accordance with the requirements as described in Section 1 and in Chapter 3 in this section. Construction logic and estimates of activity durations and material delivery lead times will have been let out before the schedule has been formulated, and the required sequences and estimates can and should be secured directly from the respective party. If modifications are subsequently required to maintain the compatibility of the subcontractor's work with the rest of the project, those variables are worked out under the auspices of that subcontractor. The resulting revised constraints will have then again come straight from the proverbial horse's mouth; all parameters should then be realistic and the probability of the acceptable performance within those parameters is good. The subcontractor will be comfortable in signing off to those commitments, and project management can proceed to schedule interdependent activities with confidence. At this stage, it is possible to submit a preliminary Mini-MOST to the subcontractor, in order to allow mobilization and coordinated start up.

The more common situation, unfortunately, (except for those projects which include a large percentage of pre-filed sub bidders) is that because of the practical requirement for the earliest possible schedule preparation, many subcontracts and purchase orders may not have been executed yet. The schedule constraints and parameters must then require that much more care in their assembly and consolidation and their maintenance of a sense of reality. The good side of this coin is that the schedule constraints can then become a part of subsequent negotiations and be pinned down in the subcontracts and purchase orders themselves as definite conditions.

It is important to realize at this stage that the concept of timely notice is not a magic formula that is taken care of at the beginning of the project and then not worried about until the eventuality of a claim. Rather, the idea of timely notice as we're using it, with repect to the MOST construction schedule, is a process that endures throughout the life of the project. It is evident with each schedule revision. As briefly discussed in Chapter 3, one fundamental requirement of construction schedules if they are to remain a legitimate representation of reality is that the periodic updates be consistently completed. This is a recognition by the courts that not only is the consideration of all variables during the schedule preparation a complicated process for any scheduling technique, but also the fact that the distinct probability exists that many of those same variables are likely to change at some point. The schedule revisions, then, along with all corresponding notice requirements must be updated to accurately reflect reality.

Apparently, the body of law surrounding construction schedules has not yet been consolidated into a single philosophy, possibly because of the dynamic nature and rapidly changing atmospheres and attitudes of the construction industry. Different courts in different circumstances have generally supported one of two views of construction schedules and the applicability of all forms of notice contained therein.

The first concept is that the constraints contained in the schedule are firm commitments; delivery dates and rates of production are to be considered as absolute. This attitude, while convenient from a record-keeping standpoint, is not in concert with the more consistently applied idea of the requirement for periodic revision. After all, if revisions are to be completed to indicate true progress with respect to reality, do we really want the old commitments to apply? That could lead to an even bigger mess.

The second philosophy, then, is the one that seems to fit more easily and with less contradiction to the idea of periodic revisions. This is the concept that the construction schedule is a guide, and not necessarily a catalog of absolute commitments. This is not to be thought of as a loose interpretation, but instead, all parties to the contract must recognize to varying degrees that it is incumbent upon _them_ to review the periodic revisions with respect to any changing requirements, fully realizing that this is simply the nature of the business, and, notwithstanding any earth shattering differences, modify their activities to conform to the current status of the project. It is this general idea which underlies the kind of continual notice that the MOST schedule will allow, without burying you in paperwork.

THE NOTIFICATION PROCESS

The first activity in the "notice" continuum is to distribute the baseline construction schedule to all subcontractors and major

EXHIBIT 2

LETTER TO SUBCONTRACTORS AND SUPPLIERS
REGARDING BASELINE SCHEDULE ACKNOWLEDGMENT

Date   Re: (Project Designation)

Subcontractor #1
Subcontractor #2   Subj: Baseline Schedule
Subcontractor #3   Acknowledgment

Gentlemen:

Attached are two copies of the Baseline Construction Schedule dated (insert date) indicating your items of work and their relations in the project. Most of the information has been supplied by your respective offices and coordinated with the project requirements.

Note that the omission here of any item called for in your contract does not relieve you of the responsibility to comply with the requirement.

Please review the schedule, paying particular attention to:

* Shop drawing submittal dates.
* Material delivery lead times.
* Activity durations.
* Dependencies (i.e., items by other trades required to be completed before your activity(ies) can be completed).
* Logic (correct sequence).

If you require any modifications to the schedule, note same in red on the schedule and immediately return it to my attention.

If the schedule as represented is acceptable to you, please indicate your acceptance and acknowledgment that your company can work within those realistic parameters by signing one copy of the schedule and returning it to me. Retain the other copy for your records.

As time is of the essence, no response by (insert date) constitutes acceptance of this Baseline Schedule by default.

                                                           Closing

cc: Owner w/att.
    Architect w/att.
    Superintendent w/att.

suppliers who have been signed on by that date. As previously noted, it is their information which had been solicited and used in the schedule (insofar as practical) mentioned in Exhibit 2, the Letter to Subcontractors and Suppliers Regarding Baseline Construction Schedule Acknowledgment. It is this fact that is the first important idea highlighted. This written recognition helps prompt the respective parties to review the schedule immediately to confirm the facts or correct any errors. The letter will be one of the first written correspondences between your offices. What is being transmitted right at the start, then, is that all information given by the subcontractor is taken at face value; it is acknowledged to have been professionally prepared, but most importantly, it is being recorded and depended upon by many organizations and individuals. The entire Baseline Schedule (not simply a Mini-MOST) is transmitted. This is to be sure that the subcontractor realizes and has been notified of all interdependencies and that your organization will not run the risk of errors and omissions.

In the case of all subcontracts and purchase orders let out after the release of the Baseline Schedule and at any point during the life of the project, their activities must be tied by the purchasing department to all production requirements. A standard condition in all subcontracts and purchase orders which directly requires all performance to be coordinated with the current construction schedule should always be included. This binds the party and places the burden on that organization to be aware of and comply with the requirements. As a practical matter, however, it is advisable to review the current MOST revision and project status with the representatives of the company being considered to clearly present and confirm all understandings of specific delivery, installation, and paperwork criteria to be met, and to be certain that that organization fully realizes that these criteria are the conditions of the order (non-compliance is then a breach of contract). These deadlines and other performance factors can be specifically included in the final written agreement, the execution of which would be the confirmation of all understandings.

The Letter to Subcontractors and Suppliers Regarding Schedule Acknowledgment transmits the preliminary schedule and secures the acknowledgment necessary to allow the preparation and issue of the final Baseline Schedule.

After all acknowledgments as outlined above are secured, the final Baseline Release (Revision A) is distributed as the confirmed realistic game plan to be depended upon by all. Copies will also be displayed in the project field office. Except under special circumstances, this is generally the last time that the entire schedule will be physically distributed to all companies (this may

EXHIBIT 3

LETTER TO SUBCONTRACTORS AND SUPPLIERS
REGARDING BASELINE SCHEDULE RELEASE

                                        Re: (Project Designation)

To: Subcontractor #1   Subj: Construction Progress
    Subcontractor #2   Schedule Final
    Subcontractor #3   Baseline Release

Gentlemen:

Attached is the (date) Baseline Construction Progress Schedule as approved by your office in its preliminary form on (date).

This schedule will be periodically updated by this office to accurately reflect current progress.

The current schedule will <u>not</u> be periodically sent to your office, but rather, it is the responsibility of all subcontractors to review these updates which will be posted at the General Contractor's jobsite office. Your office will receive copies of the Schedule Analysis/Evaluation Report for each respective revision.

Your failure to review the current construction schedule at the jobsite, or the Analysis/Evaluation Report will not relieve you of the responsibility for any and all information, obligations, project requirements, or associated liabilities contained therein.

Please acknowledge by signing below, and returning this letter to this office.

Thank you for your cooperation.

                                                                   Closing

Signature:_____

Date:_____

Name:_____

Company:_____

cc: Superintendent

change during any problem period, expediting effort, etc., as management deems appropriate).

Exhibit 3, the Letter to Subcontractors and Suppliers Regarding the Baseline Schedule Release, transmits the final document and notifies the recipient that the schedule will be periodically updated, and the current impact on all activities will be displayed at the project office. It states very clearly that it is the responsibility of the respective subcontractors to be on the site often to review the document. It is incumbent upon _them_ to be aware of all constraints, together with any modifications that may have occurred. In no uncertain terms, the parties are notified that they remain totally responsible for all posted information - ignorance is no excuse. It therefore makes good sense for them to consistently pay all required attention to the project, maintain open and clear lines of communication, and exercise the discipline to insure that all work remains properly coordinated. Finally, this notification is consummated by securing a signature from the individual authorized to commit that organization.

Unfortunately, it is only the naive contractor who will rest easy at this point, secure in the belief that once all such confirming signatures are obtained, everyone will automatically do their homework, process the paper, work out their problems, and perform these efforts in a coordinated manner and on time. Although it may be unfortunate, project managment must realize that the probability does exist, to whatever degree, that the performance of any party may falter, whether intentionally, through neglect, or unintentionally. Differences exist in levels of sophistication, organizational structures, efficiencies, and effectiveness. The profit pictures on each individual subcontract will be different, so motivations will be different. Business philosophies and individuals' capacities, experiences and authority will be different.

For these and many more reasons, project management must get and keep practical control over project momentum in addition to the legal controls of proper notifications and documentation.

To maximize the usefulness of MOST, project meetings should be arranged on a periodic basis in which all subcontractors meet at the site specifically to review performance and coordinate in detail the work of the next period. This review should be weekly during periods of critical sequences, complicated interactions, or problem areas (get-well plans), and less often if the pace of the job is smooth and problems are minimal. The MOST Construction Schedule will now become the focal point of each production meeting. It will become the mechanism that will organize discussions and clear misunderstandings.

The updating information, as discussed in Section 1, is secured from each individual at the meetings, immediately reviewed with all other meeting participants to determine the impact of any problems, and noted on the schedule. It is at this point that the dates are highlighted, get-well plans and other commitments are confirmed, and understandings of impacts and responsibilities are clarified. In this way, all information that will appear on each MOST revision will be accurate, clear, and nothing more than a confirmation of previous discussions. Its legitimacy is powerful; all statements are easily verified and supported, and each party will have been practically and formally notified of all requirements at the earliest possible stage.

It is not difficult to see, then, that consistent absences and/or casual attitudes on anyone's part cannot be tolerated. The attendance at the meetings of all subcontractors affected is not just a good idea - it should be mandatory. Unacceptable participation should not be taken lightly. As an aid to assist management to compel problem subcontractors to improve such performance, it would be helpful to have the requirement of production meeting attendance included as a written condition in the original subcontract. Non-performance is then a breach.

All these actions on the part of project management are instituted and effected to support the underlying notion that all parties to the contract must have all information required to properly coordinate their work in a timely manner. That information must be in a form that is clear for all to understand. All records with respect to that information must be organized, easily retrievable, and cataloged to support claims and backcharges. The information must also be distributed in sufficient time to responsibly allow all this.

Again, the fundamental purpose and underlying reason for all this effort is not to pin people and companies to the wall, but simply to maximize your controls to help you get the job built as planned. The safeguards outlined to compel performance and to document and support claims are not there to place claims in a priority position with respect to the schedule format. Rather, thorough assimilation of all such data in the project record is nothing more than an exhibition of professionalism and plain good business.

This brings us to the Schedule Analysis/Evaluation Report.

The Construction Schedule Analysis/Evaluation Report Shown in Exhibit #4 is, in effect, a letter of transmittal to upper management which summarizes and highlights successes and/or problems in each current revision. This is not to be confused with the Analysis/Evaluation Report described in Section 1. Instead, it is to be

EXHIBIT #4

SCHEDULE ANALYSIS/EVALUATION REPORT

To:_____   Project No:_____

_____   Title:_____

_____   Report Date:_____

                                  Revision:_____

                                  Prep. By:_____

SCHEDULE DESIGNATION			
#COPIES	REV.	DATE	REVISION TITLE/DESCRIPTION

STATUS:

As of   /   / , this project is   working (calendar) days ahead (behind) schedule, due to:

_____
_____
_____
_____

REMARKS:

_____
_____
_____
_____

cc: _____   Signed:_____

_____

considered as an optional, more detailed treatment. It is an expression of the overall performance of the project from those people who are most intimately aware of that condition - project management. The first part of the form is simply the project designation and description. The "Status" section highlights those areas (that should be included in the delay notes) which are major causes for the current state of the project. Be sure to include names, companies, and dates. Be as specific as possible. The importance of this level of detail will become evident later.

In the "Remarks" section, indicate all new constraints and conditions. If the project is doing well (on or ahead of schedule), meaningful notes might report such things as:

1. The level of confidence that project management has in the ability of the project as a whole to maintain that performance.

2. Specific critical areas that require direct attention to maintain the status.

3. Rough extrapolation of the performance into the future periods, if other known effects exist that have yet to have their impact on the project.

4. Any significant facts, proceedings, etc. which might impact the status on the next revision.

If the project is in an unacceptable status (behind schedule) include detailed outlines of:

1. All confirmed commitments, promises, etc., relative to any get-well plan devised to this point.

2. Non-performance, inattention, inappropriate actions, etc., on the part of subcontractors, suppliers, architects, engineers, the owner, etc.

3. Previously "uncritical" items which have become critical.

4. Specific action(s) required by whomever.

Again, names and dates will nail it down. In addition, references to all appropriate correspondence will ease the burden of consolidating the respective files if and when necessary.

Forward a copy of the report to all parties referenced in any way

MOST AS TIMELY NOTICE OF DAMAGES, BACKCHARGES, AND CLAIMS

in the "Status" and "Remarks" sections, and in any case, to the owner, design professionals, and to all major subcontractors on the site such as plumbing, HVAC, electrical, structural steel, and roofing subcontractors, if they apply.

This periodic distribution of the MOST schedule to the job site and of the Schedule Analysis/Evaluation Report directly to the individuals and companies as required will generally fulfill the procedural requirements that will support the value of the MOST schedule as legitimate, timely, and complete notice of all project requirements. Each incident highlighted and each delay note included will have the appropriate correspondence and files to support and detail the subject, but it is the consistent inclusion in the schedule and incorporation of the summary information that will clearly and accurately display their interrelationships, the effects on planned progress, and the usually complicated network of the chronological histories of cause and effect.

THREE

MOST Controls on Resources to Cut Direct Costs

5
Simplified Manpower / Cost Management

No project analysis is complete without a detailed consideration of manpower and costs. Manpower and cost can be applied to the MOST schedule to assist management in estimating, budgeting, and controlling costs. Manpower requirements are designated in man-days, -weeks, or -months, depending on the duration of the project.

Knowing the manpower requirements, we convert them into cost and summarize the total project cost. One big advantage of the manpower loading schedule is that, when team members are assigned other projects and their time is limited, the most efficient use of manpower can be determined.

Cost information is sometimes best applied to summary or small project schedules, because estimated costs for all the many detail jobs of a complex schedule can often be too cumbersome and confusing for meaningful analysis. Making job estimates requires the following considerations:

a. Length of job.

b. Number of personnel and their skills.

c. Man-hours per week/per month.

d. Commitments (hardware, equipment, etc.).

e. Overhead rates.

f. Indirect charges.

g. Other burdens.

In construction scheduling, manpower requirements for the general contractor are prepared by the estimators who are concerned with skilled workers, such as carpenters, masons, millworkers, helpers, laborers, and any other skilled labor not assigned to the subcontractors. The individual trades prepare their manpower requirements in much the same way as the general contractor. The skill requirements for the general contractor will be demonstrated and illustrated. The other trades can follow the same technique. In any event, it will become clear that this technique can not only be applied to all trades that will be employed on a given project, but can be applied to any business with the same usefulness.

Many estimators establish the manpower skill requirements during the bid-proposal phase and do not update or revise them during the progress of the project. The manpower will vary once the project is in operation due to:

* Underestimates.
* Weather.
* Availability of material.
* Slipping progress.
* Availability of skills.
* Trade strikes.
* Other casues.

Not many in the construction business track manpower on a timely basis. While it is true that this is usually because previous systems for doing so are complicated, confusing, and expensive, the lack of some kind of attention in this area leads to override in costs. The information is generally logged and documented when it is too late.

The information in this chapter will explain the MOST system's ability to manpower load and level, to convert to simple denominator for ease in costing, and to provide a visible presentation which will assist management in determining when and how many different types of skills are needed in advance for each project.

MANPOWER LOADING

When applied to MOST schedules, manpower requirements may be designated in man-days, -weeks, or -months depending on the duration of the project and the preference of the manager. If manpower loading is to appear on a schedule, the manager and planner must consult with team members to obtain the number of people needed in each department for each job. The planner will use this data to record manpower loading.

SIMPLIFIED MANPOWER / COST MANAGEMENT   113

In Figure 5-1, for example, "Design Tooling", which has been estimated for completion in three weeks, will take three direct-charge people working full time during a five-day, forty-hour week. No procurement personnel are required because procurement in this instance is considered overhead. Manpower loading is noted on the schedule above each job bar in the Figure. Where no direct manpower is required, it is helpful to put a zero in parentheses (0) to show the schedule user that this item has not been overlooked.

After applying the number of personnel needed to the schedule, the manager and planner must determine the number of man-weeks required. Man-weeks is the ratio of workers to the number of hours they work in a week. For example, if two people work four days of a work week, the total man hours is calculated by multiplying the two men by the number of hours, then dividing by 40 hours/week.

$$\frac{2 \text{ men} \times (8 \text{ hrs.} \times 4 \text{ days})}{40 \text{ hrs./week}} = \frac{64}{40} = 1.6 \text{ man-weeks}$$

	35	34	33	32	31	30	29	28	27	26	25	24
						(3)	(3)	(3)	0	0	0	0
						⌐DES TOOLING⌐			⌐BUY TOOLING			
				(.8)	(3)	(3)	(3)	(3)	(3)	(3)	(3)	(1.2)
				⌐	SHOP	DWGS	#3					
	(4)	(4)	(4)	(4)	(4)	0	0	0	0	0	0	0
	⌐SHOP	DWGS	#1	⌐APPR			⌐DEL⌐					
TOTAL	4	4	4	5.8	7	6	6	6	3	3	3	1.2

MANPOWER LOADING

Figure 5-1

If the two people work a five-day, forty-hour week, the total time is two man-weeks. To convert from man-weeks to man-months, the fraction in the example cited would be changed to 64 over the average work hours in a month (160 hours average per month).

"Drawing #3" in Figure 5-1 starts on the third day of the 32nd week. Three people are needed full time for the three days of that week. The manpower for that detail during that week is 1.8 man-weeks. This requirement, and the four people needed for "Drawing #1" detail during the same week total 5.8 man-weeks.

MANPOWER LEVELING FOR MAXIMUM EFFICIENCY

In Figure 5-1, three people per week have been estimated for

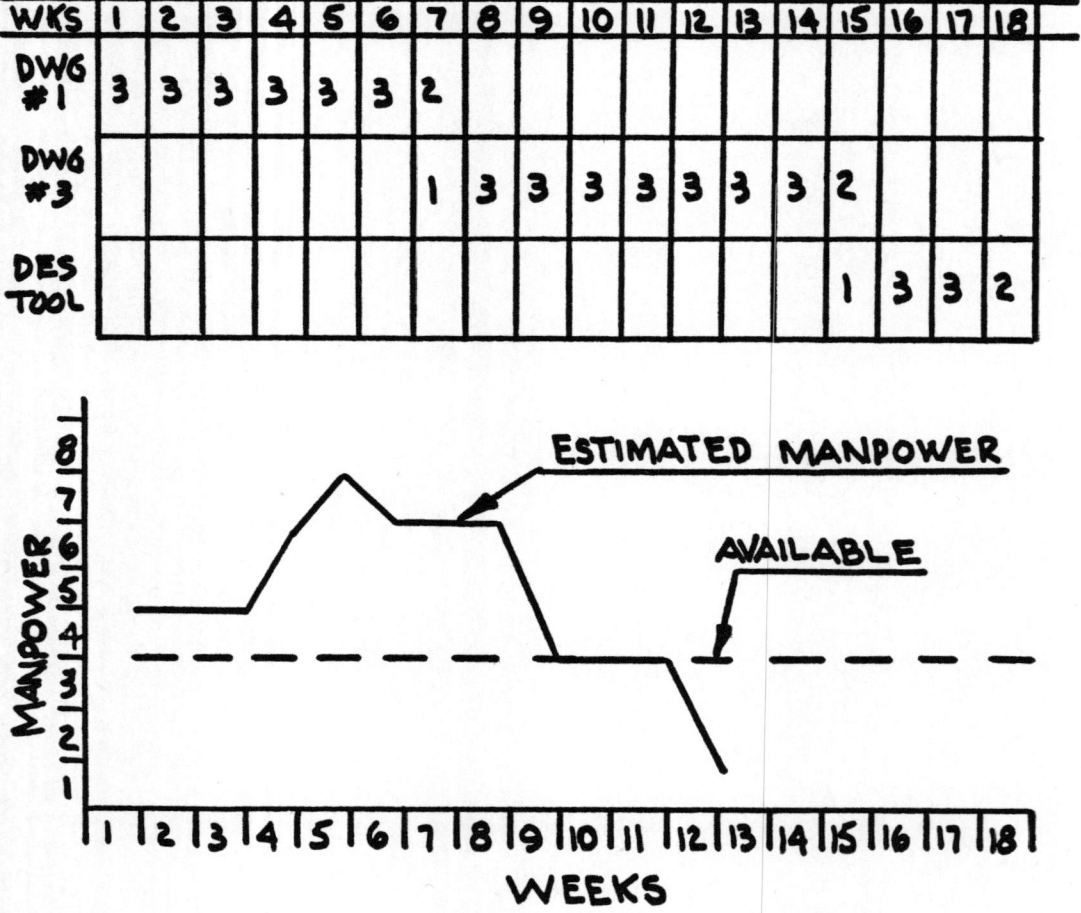

MANPOWER LEVELING

Figure 5-2

SIMPLIFIED MANPOWER / COST MANAGEMENT   115

"Drawing #3," three for "Design Tooling," and four for "Drawing #1." These jobs will take 11.4 weeks. If only three people are available for all of these jobs, the manager must extend the schedule from 11.4 weeks to 18 weeks. Revising the schedule to fit available manpower or a more desirable manpower distribution is known as manpower leveling. This is shown in Figure 5-2.

Obviously, the simplified examples in this section represent overall manpower only. For detailed estimation and control, the manpower may be broken down into varied skills. Note, however, that this is not the overwhelming calculation that it may appear to be because your are concerned only with those activities on the schedule in which you have your own direct manpower involved. For a general contractor, this often boils down to about 20% of the work.

Once the manpower leveling (a good estimate) has been established, a change in the schedule may become necessary. This change may alter the end date. It is best to know this before the Baseline Schedule takes effect. Timely monitoring of manpower leveling will help the user in knowing whether cost is affected (more about this later).

This manpower technique of MOST can be displayed on the same schedule used as the baseline. The overall "police dogging" of a construction schedule will help bring and complete the project on schedule while keeping within cost.

6

MOST / COST
for Easy Budgeting and
Cost Control

Project costs can be applied to a schedule to assist the user in estimating, budgeting, and controlling costs. Cost information is best applied to summary or small project schedules, because entering estimated costs for all the many detail jobs of a complex schedule would be cumbersome and confusing, and not really add any value to the analysis. To put it another way - you can kill a fly with a sledge hammer, and while it may be effective, it is not efficient.

As noted in Chapter 5, making job allotment estimates requires the following considerations:

* Length of each job.

* Number of personnel and their skills, for each job.

* Man-hours per week.

* Commitments (hardware, equipment, etc.).

* Overhead rates.

* Indirect charges.

* Other burdens.

With these factors analyzed, the total dollar costs can be estimated for each job. Each job's costs, entered on the schedule above each job bar, is called the allotment for that job.

If the schedule is time-phased in weeks, the allotment can be broken down into weekly estimated expenditures that are tabulated vertically. These columns can be totalled to determine estimated weekly costs.

Actual costs, as well as schedule progress, are recorded on the schedule at the updating time. After updating, the manager can compare estimated allotments with actual costs. Having cost data and work progress on a schedule assists the manager in judging project performance.

In addition to estimated allotments and actual expenditure entered on the schedule, other elements of interest can be shown, such as:

* Estimated allotment.

* Open commitments.

* Actual expenditures.

* Actual cumulative expenditures.

All of the above cost elements must include overhead rates. The General & Administration fees, indirect charges, and other burdens must be included and posted at the end of the total estimate and must be kept separated.

With the cost factors entered on the MOST schedule, the project manager can use the weekly or monthly totals as department or project budgets. In this way, he or she will be able to see whether the project is overrun or underrun at the most early and convenient time.

To enter the cost on the MOST schedule, all of the costs must be accumulated for each job and posted into the box shown at the start of each job (see Figure 6-1).

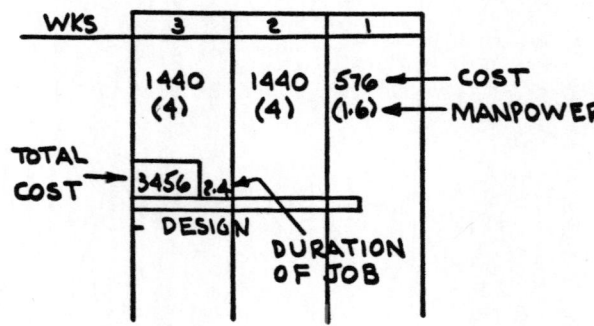

MOST/COST

Figure 6-1

The total cost for design is $3,456 covering 2.4 weeks. The $3,456 is then broken down into weekly allotments according to the manpower designations. When costs are entered for a procurement activity, the total cost for that activity is posted when the purchase is first placed. This is referred to as posting commitment. In many cases, project managers wait until the bill is paid, which is sometimes months later, but the project manager wants to be current on his or her expenditures. Therefore, by posting commitments when they are made, the manager is able to keep abreast of the project's total cost (see Figure 6-2).

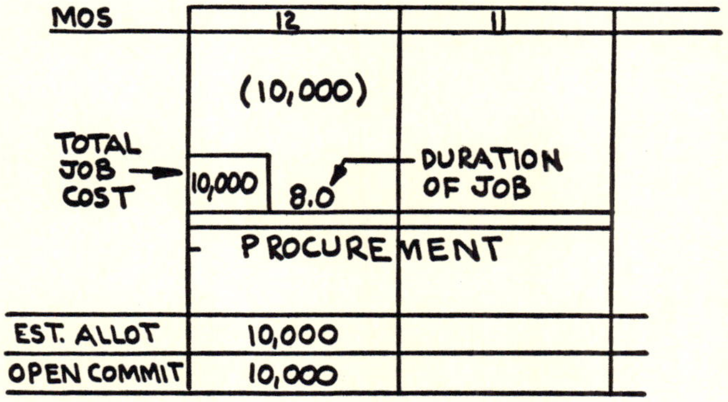

```
MOS                  |   12        |   11
                     | (10,000)    |
TOTAL JOB COST →     | 10,000  8.0 ← DURATION OF JOB
                     | PROCUREMENT
EST. ALLOT           | 10,000
OPEN COMMIT          | 10,000
```

POSTING COMMITMENT

Figure 6-2

For those jobs that are controlled by the users and those jobs budgeted by the subcontractors, the MOST/COST Tabulation shown in Figure 6-3 on the next page may be added to the bottom of the MOST schedule.

Often, tracking subcontractors' costs may be cumbersome because many are contracted to be paid for by some percentage of completion basis. In these cases, percentage curves for each subcontractor can be constructed. The "percentage of completion" can be misleading unless it is made clear if the percentage of completion includes materials and parts purchased and stored off-site, or if only on-site percentages are used.

After updating progress and posting direct costs and commitments, the inclusion of the cost in the project schedule creates weekly or monthly budgets which are monitored for overruns and underruns. This technique aids the project manager in determining not only where the project stands in relation to planned progress, but also whether he or she is spending money as budgeted.

Using MOST/COST as described above, the cost for direct labor should include overhead. Sustaining labor, such as the project manager, can be amortized throughout the project with its own

MOS	8	7	6	5
EST MANPOWER	3	14	6	8
ACT. MANPOWER	3	12		
CUM MANPOWER	3	15		
EST. ALLOTMENT	2400	20480*	16920*	17800*
CUM ALLOTMENT	2400	22880	39800	57600
ACT. EXPEND.	2400	19500		
CUM. ACTUAL	2400	21900		
OVERRIDE/(UNDER)	-	(980)		
OPEN COMMITMENT*		12000	12120	10500

← REPORTING LINE

MOST/COST TABULATION

Figure 6-3

overhead. After all direct and indirect costs and commitments including subcontractors are established, add to the total the General & Administrative (G & A), which are expenses to cover miscellaneous and administrative expenses, consultants included. Then, on top of all this, add the company profit. Prior to G & A and profit, the total costs are what the project manager must complete for management. The total cost with G & A and profit is what the project is worth to management.

7
Work Performance – Using the Status Index to Relate Actual to Planned Costs

Work performance (status index) is another project control tool that gives relative time versus dollars information. It is not only highly effective and extremely flexible, but it is also so simple that the results can be obtained by a manager, project engineer, or a secretary using a desk calculator, or even longhand.

Basically, the work performance is a means of relating actual progress and costs versus the project plan. An index of 1.0 is "par," an index above that indicates better-than-average performance for the money spent, and anything below 1.0 indicates less-than-expected progress for the amount of money spent. It provides project leaders with:

1. Time-cost performance to date in relation to the plan.

2. Time-cost projections for the completion of the project objectives.

3. A ranking of problem areas by criticality.

4. An indication of potential troublespots.

5. Anticipated schedule slippages, overruns, and underruns.

6. A means of determining where management can withdraw resources to assist more critical phases.

The index does not:

1. Provide a current project plan schedule or budget; it is dependent upon these inputs.

2. Force good, detailed planning, as MOST does. It is a useful tool in evaluating the effectiveness of planning

The index can use either MOST or milestone progress reporting

123

techniques, and provide summary and detail levels of information.

What it is:

The status index or work performance (the terms are interchangeable) is derived from the formula:

$$\frac{\text{Progress}}{\text{Scheduled Progress}} \times \frac{\text{Budget}}{\text{Actual Expenditures}} = \text{Status Index or Work Performance}$$

For instance, if the project is 10 weeks progress and should be 15 weeks per the schedule, the budget to date is $6,000, and actual expenditures are $4,000, the work performance is:

$$\frac{10 \text{ weeks}}{15 \text{ weeks}} \times \frac{\$6,000}{\$4,000} = 1.0$$

This means that although progress is behind what it should be, the progress accomplished is in line with what the cost at that point should be.

The formula is based on the relationship between the schedule and the budget. The budget is based on expenditures and commitments necessary to meet end-item deliveries and intermediate milestones. At any point in time, in other words, the planned output (progress) and the planned output (dollars) are mutually interdependent. Not that it may very likely develop that at, say the tenth-month point, one of the significant tasks is actually three months behind schedule, and that although planned expenditures are $50,000 at this point, actual expenditures are $60,000. The work performance, as an efficiency ratio, reflects this relative output and relative input:

$$\frac{\text{Output}}{\text{Input}} = \frac{7 \text{ months actual progress}}{10 \text{ months scheduled progress}} \times \frac{\$50,000 \text{ Budgeted}}{\$60,000 \text{ Actual}} = .6$$

An obvious question at this point is: "Okay, but how do you measure progress when there are a number of work efforts going on, each of varying importance, dollar value, and stage of completion?" Progress can be measured in several ways. Bearing in mind that this is intended as a management tool, one that will help the project leader determine deviations from the plan and that will show where attention is needed, progress is measured in terms of the slowest or least advanced effort under consideration. This may be measured by MOST float status or milestone status.

This measure of performance is on the conservative side because it states that if there are five weeks negative float in a project, the project as a whole is five weeks behind schedule, whereas only

WORK PERFORMANCE

the slowest task is behind by five weeks. The rest of the project may have a less negative or even positive float. These qualifications to the reported project status will appear in the Schedule Analysis/Evaluation Report as described in Section 2.

Note that it makes no difference whether the index is derived by considering the total program or the period to date as a basis, although if MOST float is used as a measure of progress, the total program would normally be considered. Using MOST float, the progress/schedule part of the formula becomes:

$$\frac{\text{Week's effort}}{\text{Planned total project time in weeks minus MOST float}}$$

If time is used:

$$\frac{\text{Week's effort}}{\text{Week's effort minus MOST float}}$$

Let's now look at the following situation in which 39 weeks' time has elapsed from July 1 to the reporting date. The Status Index for subtask #1 and each subsequent task is:

Subtask #1: $\quad \dfrac{39 \text{ wks}}{39 - (-8)} \times \dfrac{\$85,000}{105,000} = .7$

#2: $\quad \dfrac{39 \text{ wks}}{39 - (-8)} \times \dfrac{\$72,000}{186,000} = .3$

#3: $\quad \dfrac{39 \text{ wks}}{39 - 10} \times \dfrac{\$39,200}{41,100} = 1.3$

#4: $\quad \dfrac{39 \text{ wks}}{39 - 2} \times \dfrac{\$12,600}{17,400} = .8$

#5: $\quad \dfrac{39 \text{ wks}}{39 - (-8)} \times \dfrac{\$67,000}{64,000} = .9$

#6: $\quad \dfrac{39 \text{ wks}}{39 - 4} \times \dfrac{\$11,400}{14,100} = .9$

#7: $\quad \dfrac{39 \text{ wks}}{39 - 5} \times \dfrac{\$79,000}{74,000} = 1.2$

At a glance, the project leader can see how subtask #1 stands, and what tasks are in relatively good or bad shape.

Three points regarding work performance are worth noting at this time:

1. The index gives relative time versus dollar information, but does not itself indicate progress/schedule status. For instance, the progress/schedule ratio may be 1/4 and the budget/cost ratio 4/1. Then the resulting work performance is 1.0. But if the project is ten weeks behind schedule, the customer will still be unhappy, and of course, home office overhead continues, even though the project is getting its money's worth from a cost standpoint for the work done so far.

2. The budget and schedule used must apply to the identical work effort (project, task, or subtask). Otherwise, the technique cannot be applied, nor can MOST/COST or other time-cost control systems be used, for the reason that the basis for project control is lacking. This is the reason why, in Section 1 on Planning, the requirement for compatible schedules and budgets was emphasized.

3. The project leader also would like to know whether the boss is being given enough reliable progress in technical and cost at a given time.

8
MOST Financial Planning; Maximizing Investment Opportunities and Maintaining Cash-Flow

BASELINE CASH-FLOW PROJECTION

Upon acceptance and confirmation of the Baseline Construction Schedule as described in Section 2, and preferably before the general schedule of values is submitted to the owner for approval, the projected (estimated) cash-flow projection for the project life can be easily calculated.

The procedure described below can be used with many graphic scheduling techniques. The primary advantage of its use with MOST is improved accuracy, visibility, and the ability to update and correct the data. Individual projections for the work of subcontractors, the work of the general contractor, construction management fees (if applicable), expected profit dispersion, or, most simply, total project receivables, can quickly, easily and accurately be plotted. Intensive overhead, material, and labor areas will be highlighted, and the timing of receivables to payables and their amounts will be estimated and tracked.

The technique is practical, most economical, fast and accurate in its manual format. It can be programmed to work with a computer, but that is the subject of another text.

The following discussion treats the total receivable projection of a project. Any projection for the items as described above will require the identical procedure. The categories and amounts will be shifted as appropriate. Because the actual financial accounting and those ramifications are not within the scope of this book, the following procedures are confined to accounting discussion only insofar as necessary for complete treatment of the subject from the project manager's perspective.

128

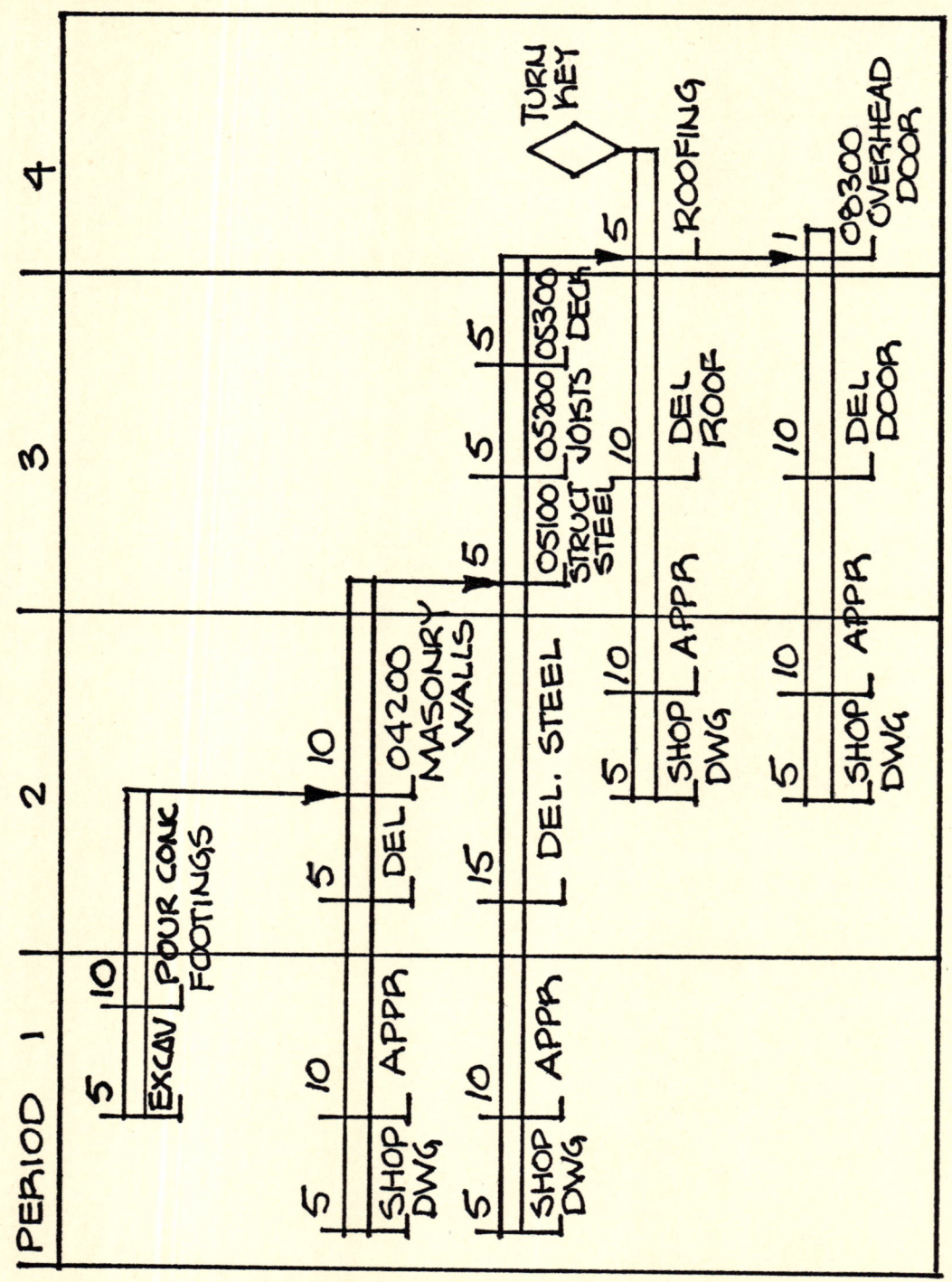

MOST FOR FINANCIAL PLANNING

Figure 8-1

MOST FINANCIAL PLANNING   129

PROCEDURE

   STEP 1

   Begin with the completed and approved Baseline Construction Schedule. Construct a grid on the schedule, segregating the individual contractual payment periods (typically months) on the horizontal scale, as in Figure 8-1.

   STEP 2

   On the <u>activity</u> portion of each bar in the category of interest, insert the <u>cost estimate</u> for that activity (note that it would be extremely helpful if the schedule activities and their respective assigned costs correlate directly with the approved schedule of values. This would not only facilitate positive comparison of the periodic requisitions for payment with the activities performed during the respective payment periods, but would also reduce or eliminate the subjective estimates of work in place, and modifications to your requisitions by the Clerk of the Works, Construction Supervisor, or other owner's agent based on whims or feelings.

   Generally, manpower and incidental materials cost estimates would be applied to the activity, unless material deliveries are

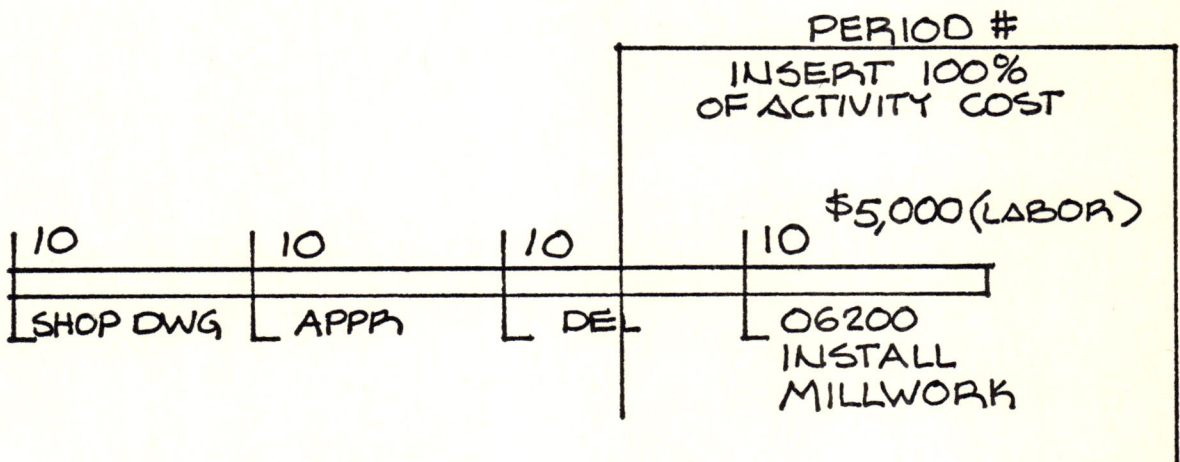

MATERIAL ESTIMATES

Figure 8-1.A

distributed throughout the period. In that case, material estimates must also be included, as in Figure 8-1.A

Many contracts (all government contracts) provide for payment of materials during the period that they are delivered physically to the jobsite, requiring that the materials be only on the site and not necessarily incorporated in the work. In such contracts, the accurate representation of the payment projection would be to include the total lump sum amount of the material cost at the end (delivery) of the material delivery portion of the schedule bar, as in Figure 8-1.B.

In any case, be sure to review the payment terms of the contract before any costs are assigned. Any and all special circumstances must then, of course, be addressed.

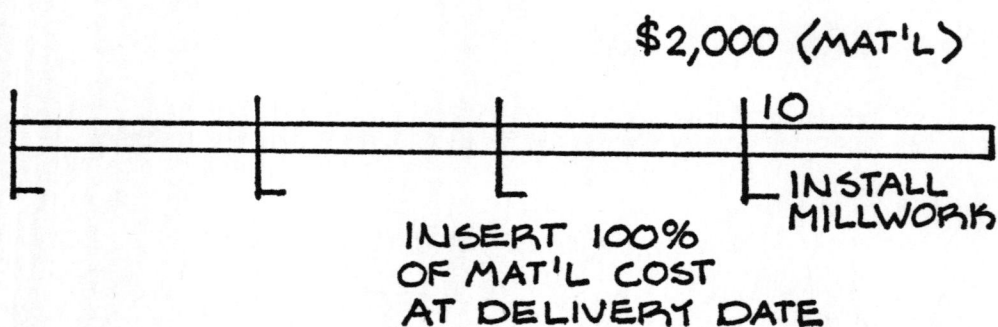

MATERIAL ESTIMATES (CONTINUED)

Figure 8-1.B

STEP 3 (Prorate)

For each activity bar that has been assigned a cost, distribute, or prorate, the cost of the bar between the separate payment periods through which it falls. Any of several methods discussed below will be appropriate for the procedure. The important thing is to first; select the method that will allow the calculation of cost disbursement in the most accurate manner for that activity, and

MOST FINANCIAL PLANNING

second; keep detailed notes on the procedure selected and the actual calculation performed _for each activity_ and file these notes and calculations with the Baseline Projection.

The value of these records cannot be emphasized enough if explanation and other support for these projections becomes necessary as is possible in negotiations, litigation, arbitration, or audit. When you have positively and quantifiably substantiated the Baseline Projection, you've taken care of the cause – the effect will take care of itself.

The case descriptions that follow will help clarify these concepts.

CASE No. 1: The entire delivery and activity falls within one (monthly) payment period.

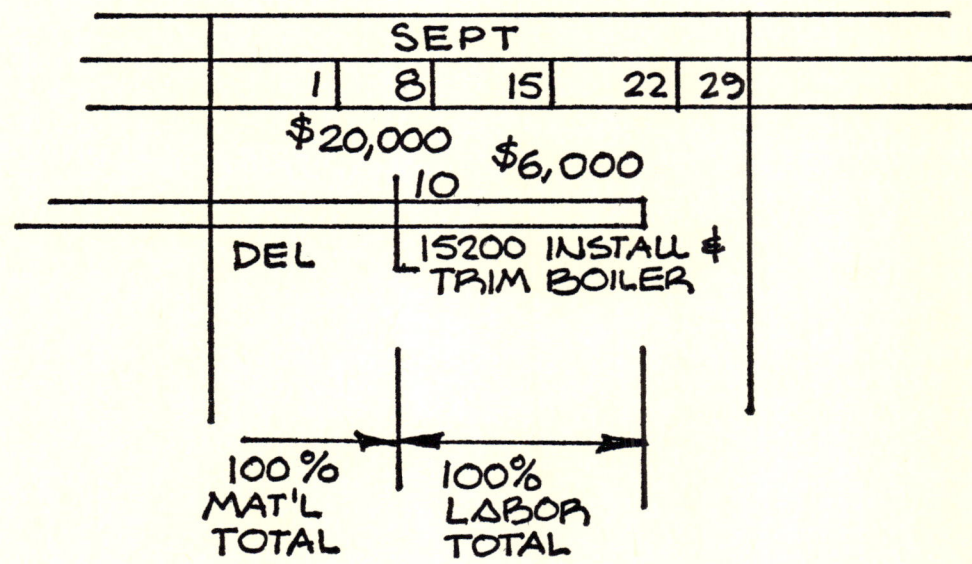

LABOR COST

Figure 8-2.A

Noting the material payment terms as discussed earlier, the payment amount as included in the approved schedule of values for the "Boiler" in the Figure 8-2.A is inserted 100% on September 11 in the example (immediately upon delivery).

Because the entire installation activity falls within the single payment period, 100% of the dollar amount ($6,000 in the example) is appropriated for that period.

CASE No. 2: The total material delivery and a consistent activity spans several payment periods, as in Figure 8-2.B below.

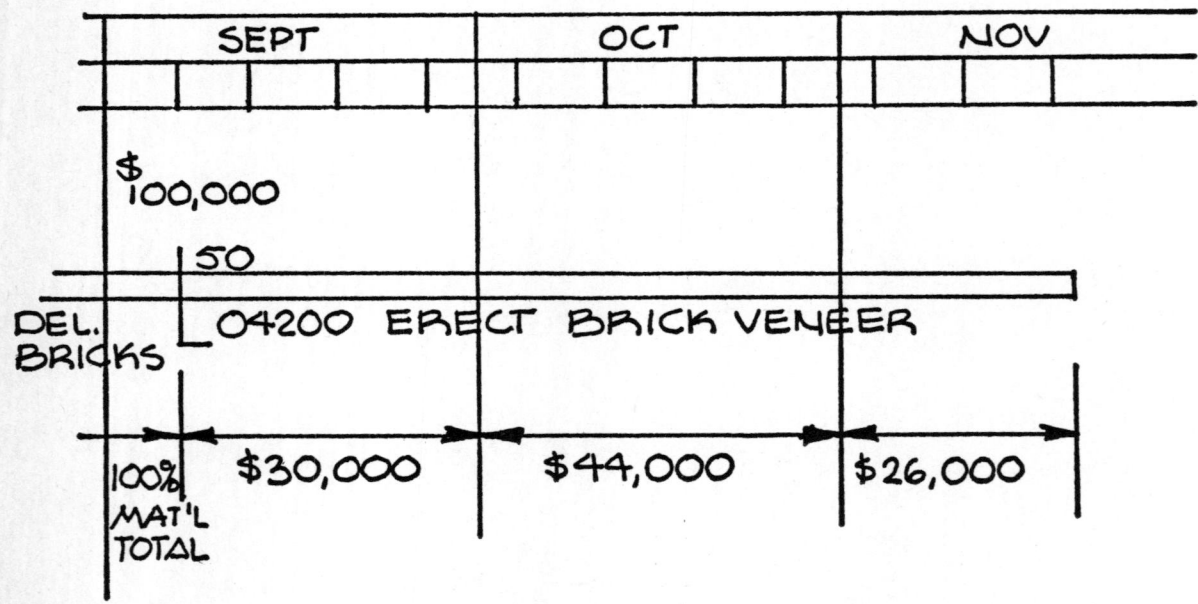

CASE No.2 - COST ASSIGNMENT

Figure 8-2.B

As in Case No. 1, 100% of the payment amount for the material (brick in this case) is inserted in September 8. Next the cost for the entire activity is prorated over the several payment periods. To do this, determine the number of working days of each activity.

MOST FINANCIAL PLANNING

and multiply that percentage by the total cost of the activity:

September: $\frac{15}{50}$ = 30% x $100,000 = $30,000

October: $\frac{22}{50}$ = 44% x $100,000 = $44,000

November: $\frac{13}{50}$ = 26% x $100,000 = $26,000

CASE No. 3: Deliver materials as a sustaining item.

In this case, material delivery, as well as the activity, spans several payment periods, as in Figure 8-3.A.

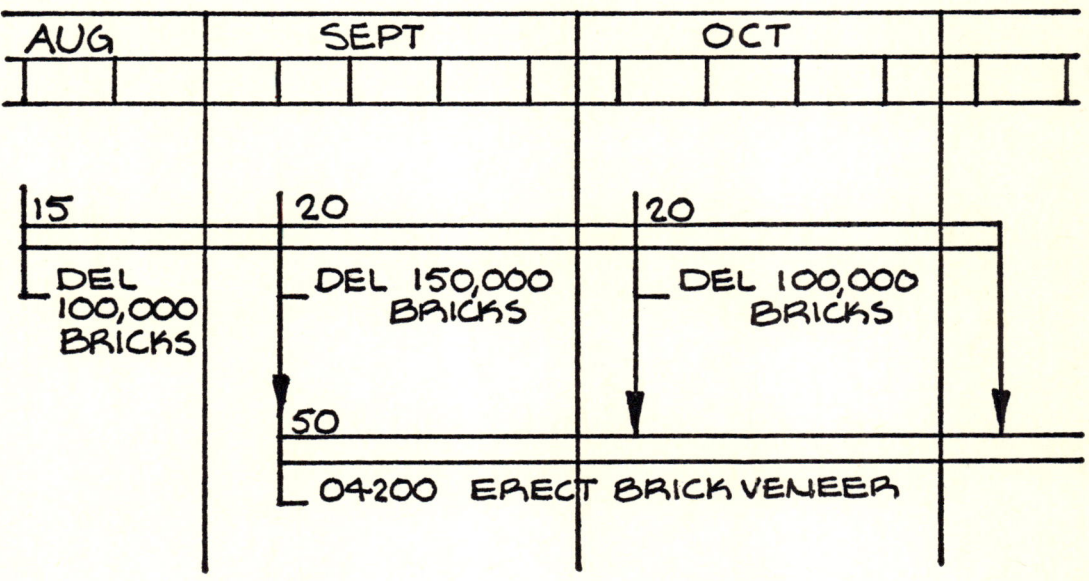

CASE No. 3 - MATERIAL ASSIGNMENT

Figure 8-3.A

In Case No. 2, the material was delivered in total in a single period and requisitioned for in that same period. More typical for either a sustaining activity, a fast-tracked sequence, or accelerated condition, the material delivery for the item may be spaced throughout the activity. The same may be true for a project with limited material storage capacity or one with a security problem.

In this case, the amount and cost of the material is estimated and, as in the single material delivery in Case No. 2, the amount to be requisitioned is included in the payment period in which the delivery actually occurs.

Note that the activity "Brick Veneer" is very general, but may be of sufficient detail and description to adequately serve the project. While it is certainly true that too detailed an activity

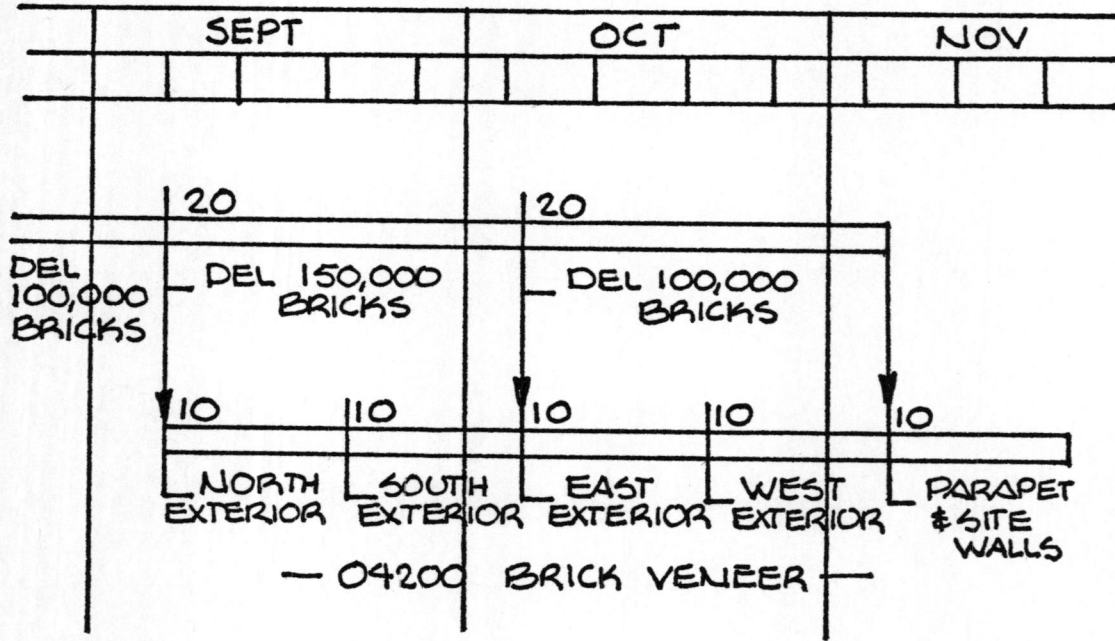

CASE No. 2 - DETAILED COST ASSIGNMENT

Figure 8-3.B

breakdown can confuse any schedule, there are many cases where a moderately detailed sequence can isolate important segments of the project and/or highlight specific potential problem areas. In that case, the more detailed sequencing will isolate more effectively the individual responsibility center.

Figure 8-3.A in a more detailed form, then, might look like Figure 8-3.B.

This is a judgment to be made at the time of the schedule preparation. In this case, Figure 8-3.A has been segregated into several activities, each of which will now be handled as in Case No. 2.

Select whichever procedure described above that is appropriate for all remaining activities on the schedule and continue until all activities have their costs accurately distributed throughout every payment period. Do <u>not</u> destroy your notes – <u>file them</u>.

STEP 4: Consolidate all costs.

Once Step 3 has been completed for each activity, total all amounts in each payment period and enter the number at the bottom of each column, as done in Figure 8-4.A.

Again, this procedure can be as detailed as appropriate. For example, material and labor can be separated, G.C. and subcontractors' work can be separated; and numerous additional combinations can be employed as you wish. Because, in a typical bid, overhead and profit are added in as a lump sum percentage after the total project costs are estimated, the same will also apply here.

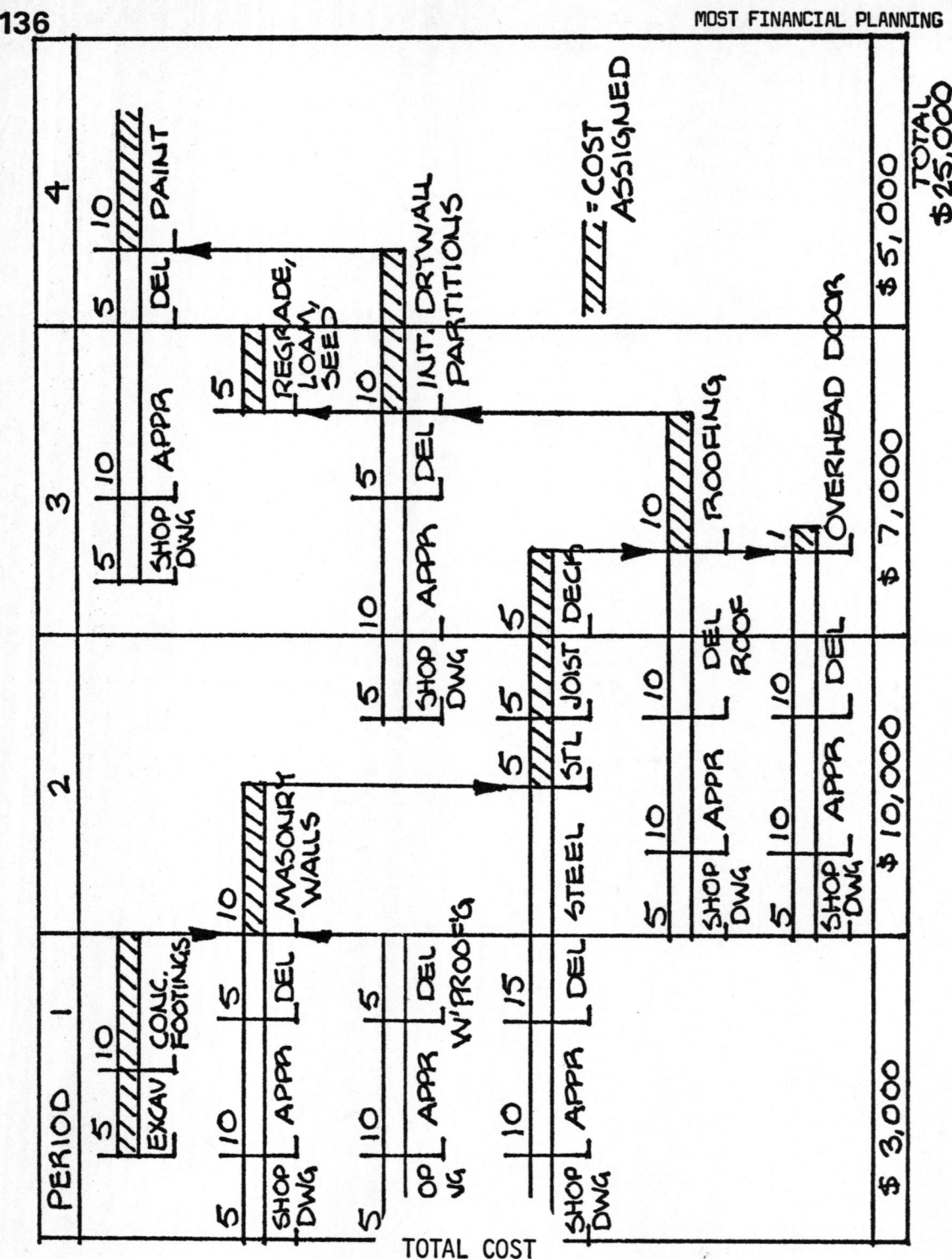

Figure 8-4.A

MOST FINANCIAL PLANNING   137

   After all total costs for each payment period are determined, calculate each period's percentage of the total project costs and prorate the overhead and profit over each period per those percentages to arrive at the total receivable for the period. Figure 8-4.B shows these calculations:

   (In this case, overhead was calculated at 10% of the receivable costs for the period, and profit was calculated at 10% the sum of cost + overhead. For example, the overhead in period 2 is $10,000 x 10% = $1,000; the profit in period 1 is ($3,000 + $300) x 10% = $330.)

	PERIOD 1	2	3	4	TOTAL
COST	$3,000	10,000	7,000	5,000	$25,000
%·PROJ	12%	40%	28%	20%	100%
OVERHEAD	$ 300	1,000	700	500	$ 2,500
PROFIT	$ 330	1,100	770	550	$ 2,750
TOTAL RECEIVABLE	$3,630	12,100	8,470	6,250	$30,450 → CONTRACT PRICE

PROJECTED RECEIVABLE TABULATION

Figure 8-4.B

STEP 5: Plot the information.

   On a sheet of graph paper, or even on the construction schedule itself if the entire schedule is on a single page, construct a graph, including the individual payment periods in the horizontal scale, and dollars ranging from $0.00 to the total contract price in the vertical scale.

   Two curves can now be plotted. First, the projected receivables for each period are individually placed on the curve. Figure 8-5.A shows such a histogram:

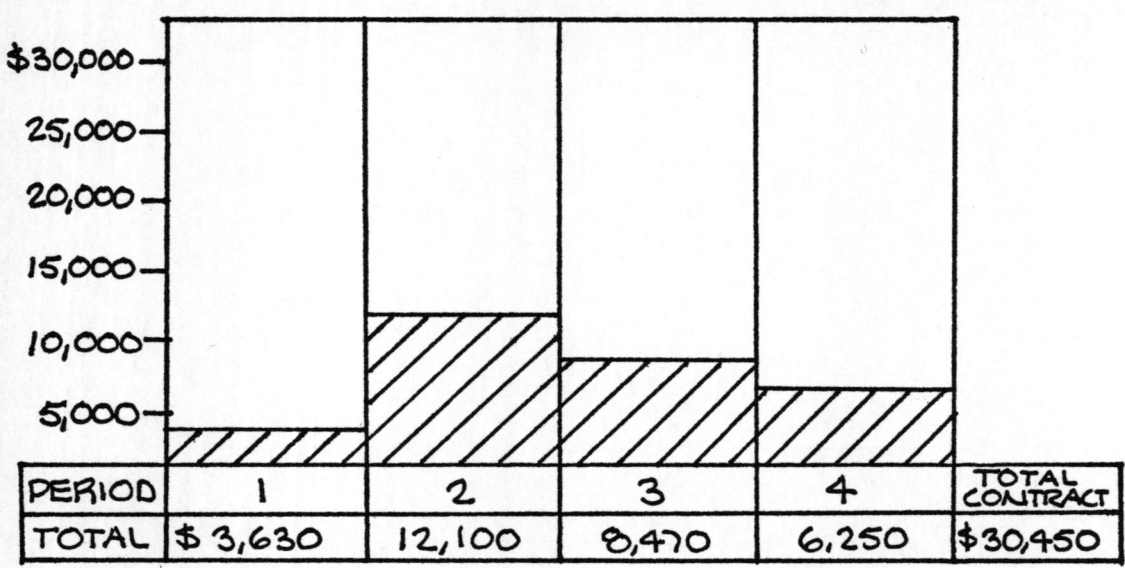

INDIVIDUAL COST

Figure 8-5.A

Next, on the same sheet or on a separate graph, the cumulative receivables will be plotted, by simply adding each period's amount to the previous total. This is shown in Figure 8-5.B:

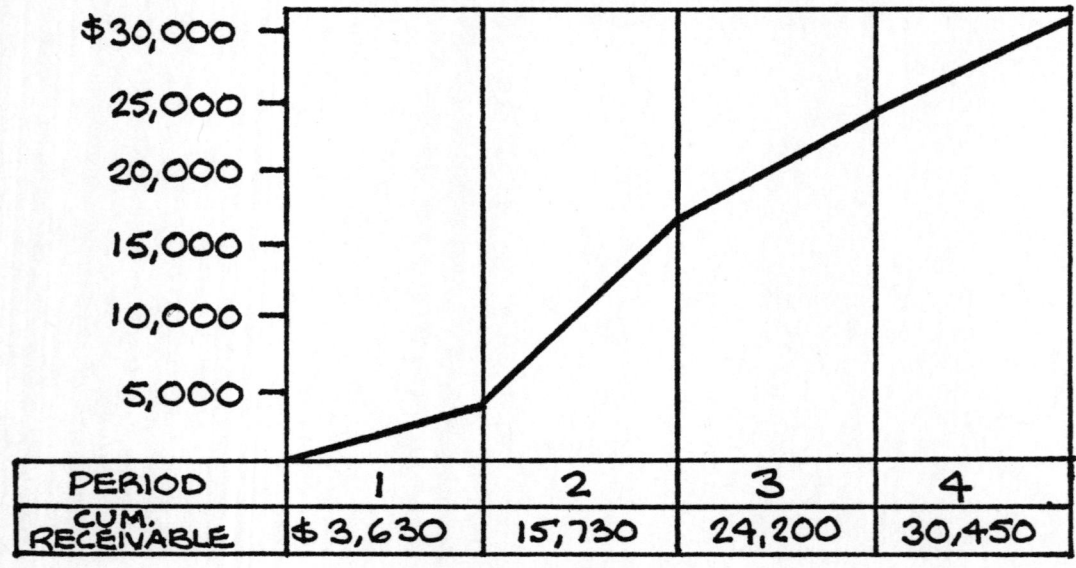

CUMULATIVE COST

Figure 8-5.B

In this simplified example with only four payment periods, the curve is abrupt, with no distinct shape. In a real detailed analysis of an entire project spanning many payment periods, the curve most often begins shallow, steepens as the job begins to gain momentum during the mid stages in its most cost-intensive phases, and flattens again towards the final phases as the relatively less expensive "finish" items occur and then trail off. This common characteristic shape has therefore resulted in term "S - Curve." (As a footnote, because this "S" shape is so common for a cumulative-type curve on properly prepared schedules, if you note that the shape of one of your curves is dramatically different, it may be an indication that the schedule is not realistic or otherwise inaccurate in the first place. There may be a perfectly good explanation for the effect, but in that case, the "S - Curve" analysis will at least force a re-review to confirm what will be an unusual circumstance.)

This completes the Baseline Cash-Flow Projection for the single project. At a glance, you now have at your disposal:

* Expected amount and timing of receivables.

* Percentages of completions.

* Projected profit disbursement.

* Projected overhead disbursement.

REPORTING AGAINST THE BASELINE CASH-FLOW PROJECTION; USES OF THE CUMULATIVE RECEIVABLE CURVE (S - CURVE)

In the discussion that follows, the use of the Receivable Curve and the techniques for reporting against the Baseline Cash-Flow Projection with respect to prime contracts, subcontracts, work of the general contractor, and change orders will be outlined. As will become evident, it may not be necessary for you to use all the curves and information that can possibly be generated. However, you will now have at your disposal a wide array of reporting procedures which can be drawn upon as each individual project or company requires. All separate projections are constructed with essentially the same procedure. The major differences lie in the particular categories of cost to include in the projection.

The prerequisites, then, to be completed before meaningful reporting can begin are:

1) The completed receivable projection and curve.

2) The selection by management of those categories of information that will be desirable to track.

What will be presented for the remainder of this section will be a demonstration of the basic technique with respect to the total receivables of the project. Because overhead and profit figures are commonly represented as percentages of the total, these numbers can be generated as a side effect.

REPORTING (PLOTTING) PROJECT STATUS

Reporting the project's status in the project's original configuration (without change orders) is accomplished by inserting the actual requisitioned dollar amounts as they occur in the appropriate respective areas at the base of the projection, and plotting those actual amounts directly on the same cumulative receivables curve.

Instantaneously, and without the need to review and decipher computer tab runs, payroll reports, and other stacks of paper, you and the rest of management will get the full, vivid picture of the financial status of the project - accurately and completely. More than just getting the "feel" of how the job is going, you will assimilate the real information quickly, totally, without bias, and most importantly, in time to do something about it. You'll get the immediate picture of not only whether the project is financially ahead, behind, or on target, but also by exactly how much.

THE STATUS LINE

Record and plot the actual information at each period as it becomes available. With each passing month, the development of the project's STATUS LINE - the comparison of actual receivables to the projected receivables - will significantly increase the total visibility - and control - of the job.

The completed plot of the "actual" information for all four periods in the previous example is shown in Figure 8-6.

By considering only the status line, and without additional entries and calculations, accurate and timely reports can be submitted to management which would answer, to a reliable degree, questions such as:

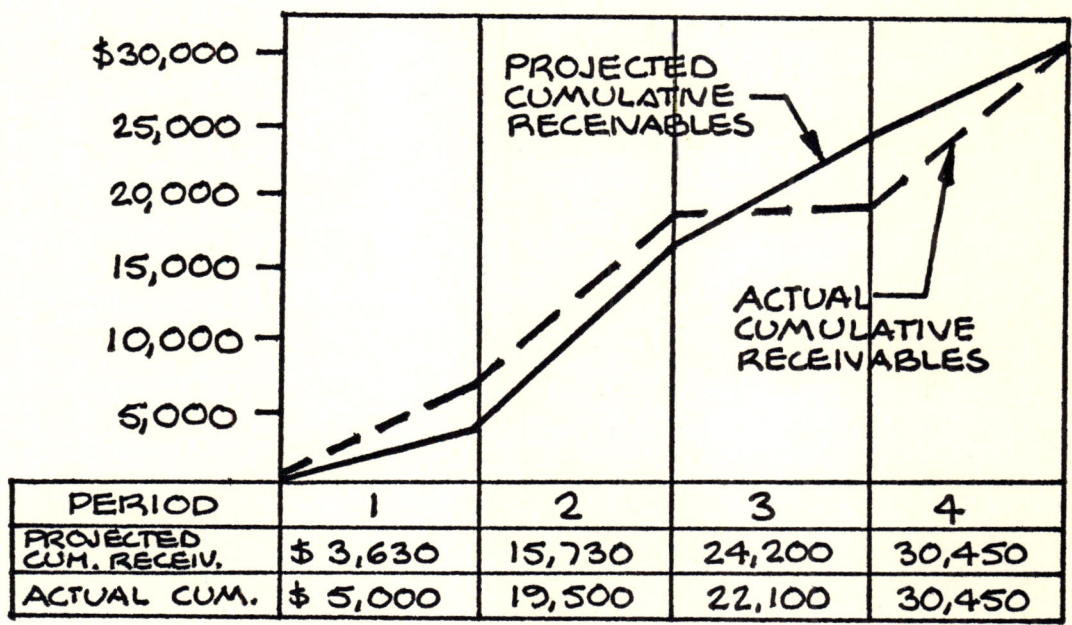

ACTUAL vs. PROJECTED RECEIVABLES

Figure 8-6

1. How are actual requisitions (costs, overhead, profit, etc.) performing in relation to that projected?
    a. Are they above, below, or on projected amounts - why?
        - Poor or exceptional performance
        - Owner cooperation or antagonism
        - Acceleration
        - Delays
        - Strike
        - Schedule sequence interruptions
        - Early or late submission of requisitions that will affect the allowability of items to be billed
        - Overbilling or underbilling, and how it will affect the next payment period (don't be lulled into a false sense of security)
        - Correct or incorrect schedule logic or durations
        - Inclusion of change order billings (more about this

later)
- Material delivery interruptions
- Overstocks

2. How does the requisition for payment trend (history) compare with the construction Trend Analysis?
   a. Are payments from the owner corresponding to improvements or delays in the project completion date - Why?
      - Delivery problems
      - Inappropriate or unauthorized increases or decreases in the approved requisition dollar amounts
      - Change orders
      - Justifications for interest payments on excessively outstanding receivables

3. Do requisition dollar amounts accurately reflect the amount of work performed (by the general contractor and/or subcontractors and suppliers)?
   a. Underbillings or overbillings - Why?
   b. Percentage of completion
   c. Early (ahead of schedule) deliveries of expensive equipment may push the billing up for the period. The percentages of dollars requisitioned for will exceed the work in place, especially if the installation is scheduled for a much later period.

4. Have change orders affected payments and/or completion of contract work?
   a. Has this effect been accounted for in the change order price?
   b. Was the effect unanticipated?
   c. Who/what caused the effect?
      - Direct schedule impact by change in specification or project requirements
      - Reworking - demolition and reinstallation
      - Delays in completing contract work because of new construction or material deliveries
      - Elimination of contract work (is a credit change order due?)

5. Are billings up/down because of exceptionally good/poor performance of (a) particular subcontractor(s) and/or supplier(s)?
   a. Accelerated or poor performance of the critical path. (Note that some combination of (a) and (b) above may give an acceptable dollar amount for the period, but the project completion date might remain in jeopardy.)

MOST FINANCIAL PLANNING   **143**

    6. What effects are being introduced to the retainage amount
       and its projected release relative to the original project
       completion date (notwithstanding change orders)?
       a. Each change order that affects the completion date
          will directly affect the scheduled release of
          retainage (as well as other contract payments).
            - Are these effects accounted for in the change order
              price?
            - Every delay in the project completion will delay
              the release of the retainage amount.

The Projected Receivable Tabulation, as was shown in Figure 8-4.B, will be expanded to include the actual status of the respective categories. Again, any or all categories can be included in the analysis, as management deems appropriate. Figure 8-7 will include status numbers (actual history) for each category previously separated. One may not require this level of detail, but the information generated as it occurs is much less time consuming, confusing, and costly to generate now, rather than an attempt to piece it together in total after the fact.

A=ACTUAL   P=PROJECTED

PERIOD	1		2		3		4	
DESCRIPTION	P	A	P	A	P	A	P	A
COST	3,000	4,132.23	10,000	11,983.40	7,000	2,148.76	5,000	6,900.82
% OF PROJECT	12%	16.4%	40%	47.6%	28%	8.5%	20%	27.4%
OVERHEAD	300	413.22	1,000	1,198.34	700	214.88	500	690.01
PROFIT	330	454.55	1,100	1,318.26	770	236.36	550	759.17
TOTAL RECEIVABLE	3,630	5,000	12,100	14,500	8,470	2,600	6,250	8,350

RECEIVABLE STATUS TABULATION

Figure 8-7

MOST FINANCIAL PLANNING

PERIOD	1		2		3		4	
	P	A	P	A	P	A	P	A
COST CONTRACT								
COST CHANGE								
COST TOTAL								
% OF PROJ CONTRACT								
% OF PROJ CHANGE								
% OF PROJ TOTAL								
OVERHEAD CONTRACT								
OVERHEAD CHANGE								
OVERHEAD TOTAL								
PROFIT CONTRACT								
PROFIT CHANGE								
PROFIT TOTAL								
TOTAL RECEIV CONTRACT								
TOTAL RECEIV CHANGE								
TOTAL RECEIV TOTAL								

COMPLETE RECEIVABLE STATUS TABULATION

Figure 8-8

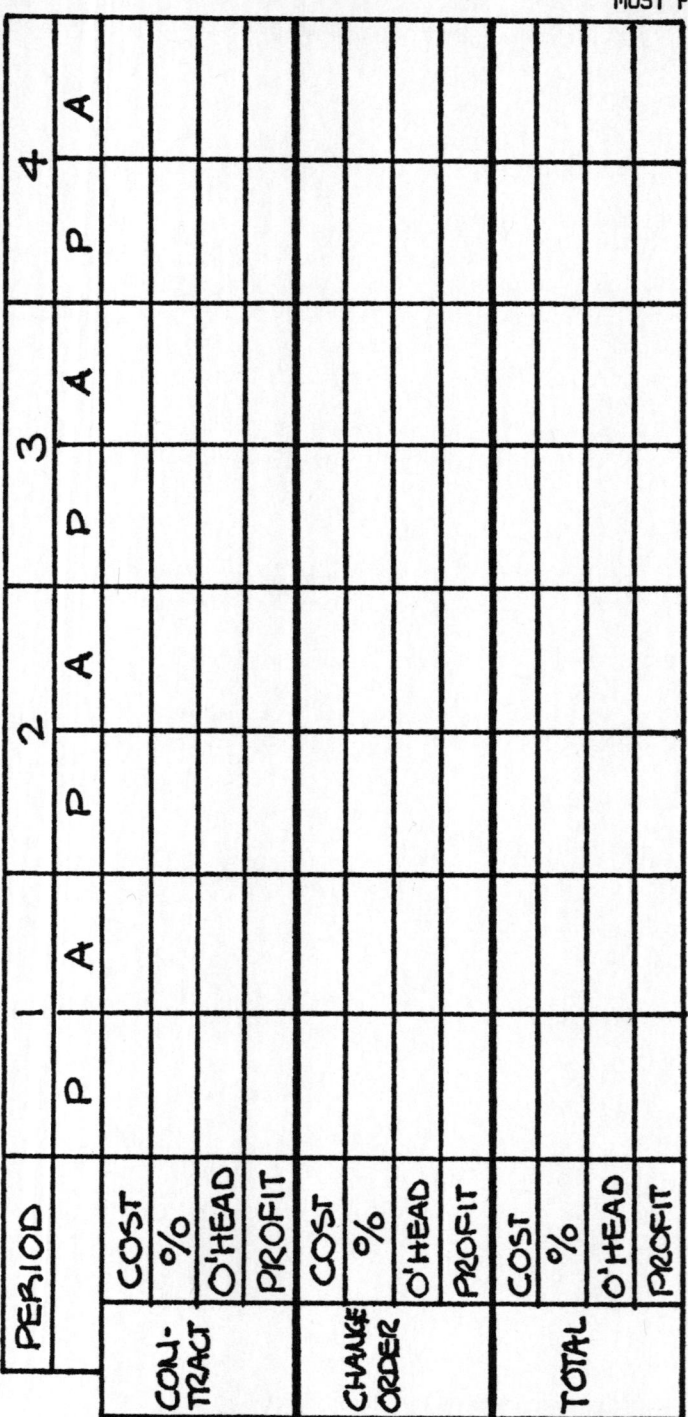

COMPLETED RECEIVABLE STATUS TABULATION
(OPTIONAL FORMAT)

Figure 8-9

REPORTING (PLOTTING) CHANGE ORDERS

To maintain accuracy in reporting the current status of original contract costs or receivables as described above, care must be taken to insure that the dollar amounts to be applied to change orders are not directly intermingled in the Status Line for contract work. If the receivables for change orders were simply attached to the original contract receivable and reported in the same line, the direct result would be inflated reports (assuming "Add" change orders) for the original work that might very well lull management into a false sense of security; the project would appear to be doing financially better that it really may be. Separation of change orders for reporting meaningful information, then, is absolutely necessary.

As change orders occur during the life of the project, their inclusion in the construction schedule as detailed in Section 2 has already definitely and quantifiably illustrated the total project impact from the production standpoint. When those change orders have been so graphically and completely introduced, their impact must then also be included in the Projected Receivable Tabulation, and their total effect on the project recorded in the Receivable Status Tabulation. The Receivable Status Tabulation will now finally expand to its complete form in the examples in Figures 8-8 and 8-9.

The projection and status for all project activities are now generally complete (as previously stated, treatment of change orders with differing effects on contract work will follow). A detailed review of the completed Status Line analysis at this point will allow concise, complete, and accurate answers to such questions as:

1. Are actual receivables progressing at the same rate as production?
    a. Does the remaining dollar amount of the contract roughly equal the remaining work to be completed?

2. Have change orders significantly affected payments for contract work?
    a. Have time extensions delayed payments for contract work into other periods?
    b. Have there been reductions in or changes to contract work?

3. Are overhead and profit dollar amounts remaining at acceptable levels (notwithstanding change orders)?

4. Are the change orders adding to the value and profit potential of the job, or are they simply interfering with the job's

systematic completion.

5. Is the release of retainage being affected?

6. Are requisitions being submitted to the owner in a timely manner?

7. Are payments being made by the owner in accordance with the terms of the contract with respect to elapsed time?

8. Are changes being made by the owner's agent in unauthorized reductions in requisition dollar amounts without proper substantiation?

CHANGE ORDER (CONTRACT MODIFICATION) IMPACT

If one or several change orders occur which are large in proportion to the original contract, the scope of the project may effectively change. This is important to be aware of because the company's projected work in place may significantly increase or decrease. Many contracts are written which provide for the owner's right to direct the contractor to include change orders, but <u>well</u> written clauses also will prevent large changes in the contract scope which will significantly affect the contractor's financial position. The basic MOST reporting technique will track the definite impact of change orders on production, but status line analysis will track and quantify the effect on receivables, the implications of which may be favorable, or highlight and support a claim for damages.

Depending upon the significance of the change order(s) and management's discretion, a corrected (or updated) total receivables projection can be plotted, but this is seldom necessary, and may serve only to complicate the analysis. To remain accurate, it will have to be replotted after each change order, which is contrary to the basic MOST philosophy of rescheduling without redrawing, with or without the revised projection. A status line for total receivables which includes the change order amounts is now easily included and distinguished from the status line for original contract work.

In the discussion that follows, two basic scheduling situations will be developed, each for change order situations having differing levels of direct impact on the project's original contract work. Their individual projections and status will be plotted on the same total status line to maintain visibility, clarity, and the ease of comparison characteristic of MOST. Each change order will be individually plotted (projected) and monitored, and their relation to

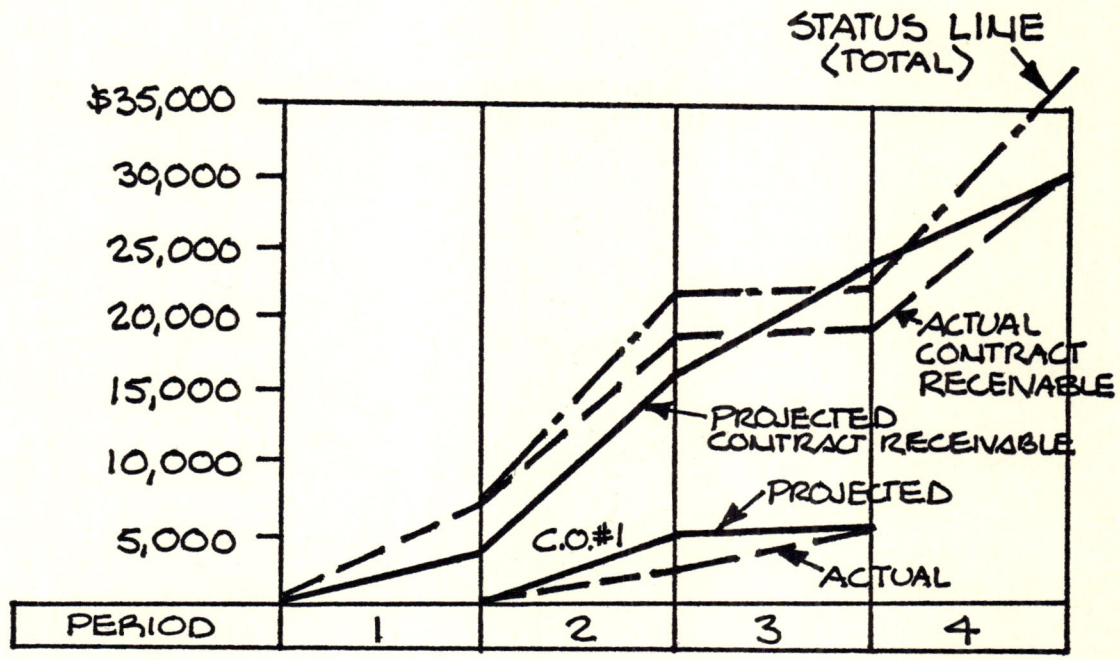

CHANGE ORDER COST

Figure 8-10

the project's performance of the original contract detailed.

TYPE 1

The first, and most simple type is the single change order of small or moderate size which is not directly or indirectly dependent upon contract activities, does not have any effect on subsequent activities, and is thus wholly independent of the original project for practical purposes. This criteria will immediately be evident if your review of the MOST schedule including the change order reveals no dependency lines, and the change order production schedule is, for practical purposes, independent.

The procedure for assigning costs to the change order activity(ies) is identical to that described in the beginning of this chapter for contract work. The individual projected dollar amounts are plotted on the same graph as the contract projected and status lines. Appropriately labeled, the isolated change order will then be easily defined and readily identified. This is shown in Figure 8-10.

After the individual projections for the contract work and the change order work are completed, the dollar amounts for the separate status lines are totalled and the result is plotted for the respective periods to arrive at the absolute status line for the project's complete work in place.

TYPE 2

In this example, the more common and correspondingly more complicated situation will be explored. The change order initiated by a design improvement or correction, changed site condition, latent defects, error, omission, delay, or any other circumstance in which contract work is interrupted and the logic, sequence, start-up, and duration of subsequent contract activities are directly affected.

Again, these details will have been quantifiably outlined in the treatment of the change order as described in Section 2, and accountability will have been documented under "Delay Notes" and in the correspondence. The costs will be assigned to the change order activities in a manner consistent with the procedure previously described and the projection for the individual change order plotted as in Figure 8-10.

The notable difference in this situation will be the direct result of reductions to or delays in projected payments for contract work. This will become most evident if the status line for contract work dips below the projected level. This effect will immediately and obviously highlight the problem area, and signal the requirement for immediate management attention through the visibility characteristic of MOST. This is shown in Figure 8-11.A:

Note that because both curves are cumulative amounts, the slopes will never become negative (point downward). Rather, the _rate_ of increase will be affected. The worst condition ($0.00 payment) will result in a flat line (no change) in the period.

Any change in the slope (rate of increase) of the status line will highlight a change from the projected rate. If the previous periods have done well with respect to the projected receivables, a decrease in the slope of the status line during the problem period(s) may not cause the status line to graphically dip below the projected curve, but the line will begin to flatten out as the rate of production and corresponding rate of payments decreases. It is this

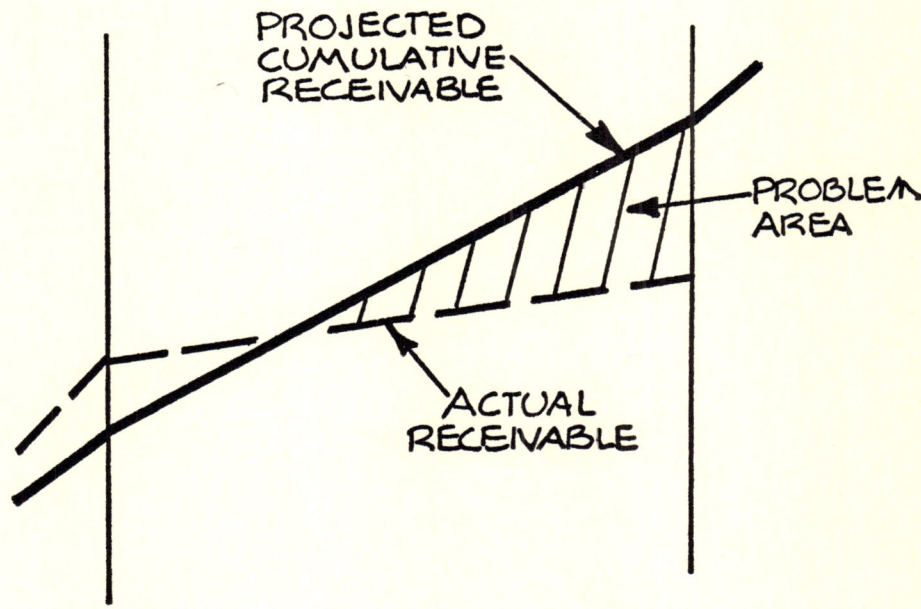

PROBLEM AREA CURVE

Figure 8-11.A

flattening out - the decrease in the percentage of slope - that is the important effect to be aware of.

In Figure 8-11.B, period 1 has done very well relative to planned performance. This is evidenced by the steeper slope of the status line, which graphically defines the greater rate of production. Period 2 has recorded an acceptable level of performance; the slope of the line is nearly equal to the slope of the projected performance line. The plotting of the status line (actual performance) is nearly equal to the slope of the projected performance line. The plotting of the status line above the projected is a definite indication to management that for the time being, the project as a whole is performing that much better than projected (because of the exceptional gain of period 1). The elevated level of total actual receivables, however, is really nothing more than a carry over of past successes. The performance in period 2, then, is only "par."

Period 3, in the Figure has a serious problem. The description, history, accountability, and get-well plans will have been defined and documented as described in Sections 1 and 2. The line here shows

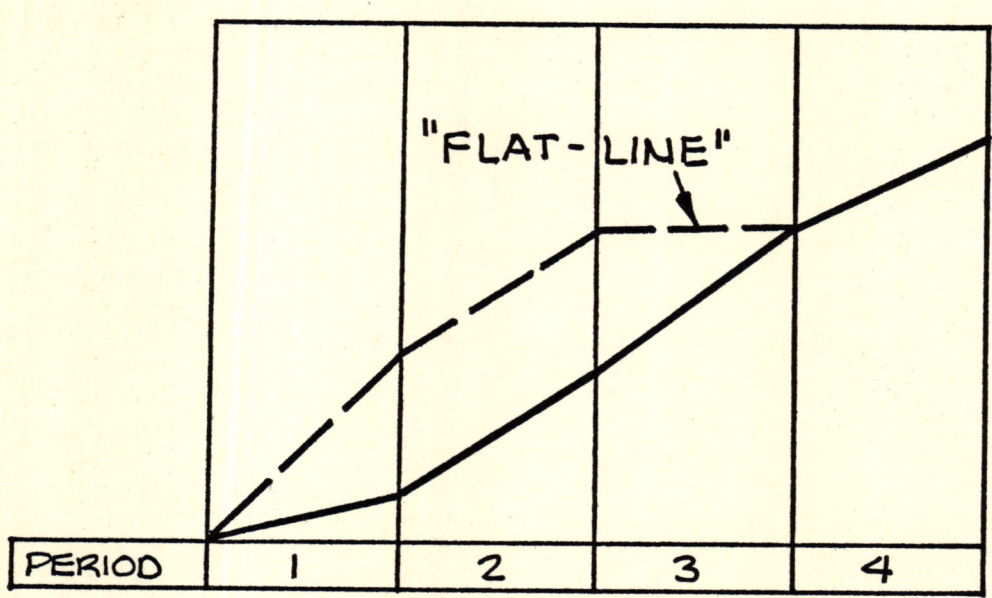

PROJECTED vs ACTUAL RECEIVABLES

Figure 8-11.B

that the rate of billable production has slowed, authorized payments have been reduced, and the status line has flattened relative to expected receivables. In the example, the absolute dollar amount of the actual receivables has remained at an acceptable level for the project as a whole (equal or greater to the planned amount for that date), but the "flat lining" of the status line is a dramatic and meaningful cue to compel management to immediately secure correct and complete answers to questions such as:

1. What caused the drop in the production rate and allowable billings (requisition dollar amounts)? (Review the project record.)

2. Is everything properly documented? (Review the Delay Notes and the correspondence.)

MOST FINANCIAL PLANNING

3. Has the problem been resolved or will other periods also be affected?

4. Even if the cause of the flat line has been corrected, do any long term effects remain?

5. Have measures been taken to insure that similar circumstances do not recur?

6. Will any residual effects impact the production and/or receivables of subsequent periods?

If the cause(s) of the flat-line effect has (have) been corrected and no reason is remaining that will prevent scheduled production rates of period 4 in the example from being achieved, the project will remain at an acceptable level. Actual status will still meet or exceed projected. If the situation, however, remains unresolved unacceptable rates of production may be forecast to future periods. The shallow slope of the flat-line will then be extrapolated to period 4.

The probability and size of such an effect and all underlying circumstances as detailed in the Delay Notes will indicate the specific delays and resulting impacts on milestones, on all completion dates, and on all immediate and long-term effects on production, together with any feasible get-well plans. This procedure and use of the status line analysis will then identify and quantify the financial impact.

The significant achievement of this technique is the dramatic increase in the usefulness of this information to management in negotiations, arbitration, and financial analysis because of the _timely_ assimilation and projection of the data - in time to take action to prevent or alter the "inevitable" consequences before they occur - not merely presenting a good explanation for a bad history.

Let's now return to Figure 8-11.B's period 1 for a moment. We observed earlier that period 1 has done well relative to projected receivables; the slope was more steep indicating greater achievement. What happens, then, in a period where production and requisition amounts are making exceptional gains, but doing so in the wake of several problem periods, as does period 6 in Figure 8-11.C.

Again, the problems' documentation and get-well plans for the example's periods 4 and 5 will be outlined as in Section 1. For clarity, our concern here is only that the flat-lining has occurred in those previous periods.

A review of the status line now seems to indicate that whatever the problem was, it now appears to have been corrected by the end of period 5, allowing the gains in production evidenced by the steep slope in period 6 to be achieved.

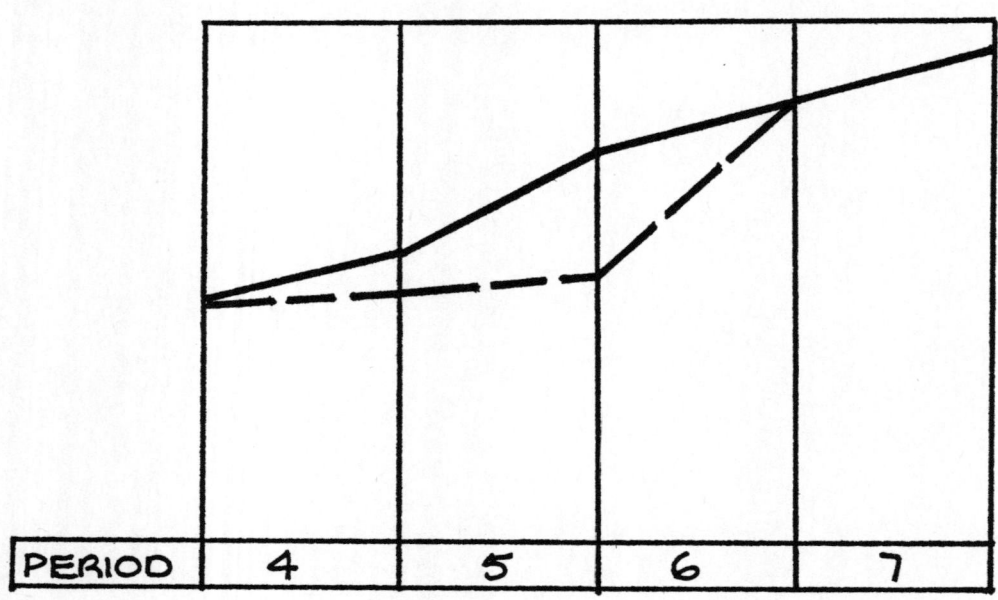

PROJECTED vs. ACTUAL RECEIVABLES

Figure 8-11.C

Note for a moment the gradually decreasing slopes in the projected line for periods 5, 6, and 7 as the project nears completion. This gradual flattening of the line for the projected receivables for the last few periods is a typical effect for nearly every project. It indicates that the big, expensive, and cost-intensive items such as the building structure, roofing and the major mechanical and electrical equipment and systems are mostly complete, and the relatively less expensive "finish" items are remaining. The important idea is that it is a predictable effect which management can depend on to a certain degree when considering such ideas as:

1. How has the stage of completion of the project affected production capacity?

2. Can resources be redirected to other projects because of the less intense production rates of this project?

3. Can the most effective personnel on this job be transferred to projects in other areas without adversely affecting this job?

Well, all these realizations and observations are fine, but how is all this going to affect the status line analysis for our get-well performance in period 6 in Figure 8-11.C? When the performance gain in period 6 is first reviewed, and management has satisfied itself that the situation has, in fact, been remedied and will not have an absolute effect on the subsequent period 7 and/or the project's completion date, the tendency may be to accept the improvement at its face value. But what may have really happened here?

Compare the slope of the status line with the slope of the projected. The status line is much steeper. Although the steepness is certainly a favorable indication from strictly a billing standpoint, as in period 1 of the previous example, there remains the possibility that a few negative barbs must be identified and resolved. Consider that now:

1. Intensive production rates have occurred in a period where management may have been relying on the release of key people for other projects because of slow projected rates.

2. Outstanding total capacity of the organization may have changed; effort must be concentrated here, with corresponding overhead, instead of being shifted into other areas - opportunity lost.

3. The steep slope may represent a forced acceleration in production which, although may have ultimately resulted in a greater receivable for the period, may have also included gross inefficiencies of manpower, equipment and materials.

The consideration of these and other issues that may become evident will help insure that all causes and effects are identified. It is this knowledge that may support claims, improve negotiations, and integrate communication within the organization, but most importantly will confirm confidently to management that all issues have been completely and competently brought to resolution - nothing has been missed, and no loose ends remain.

THE MAXI-MOST INTEGRATION

General Overview

The Maxi-MOST integration is basically the combination or total net effect of all projects into a complete organizational projection of production and receivables. It is the integration of the projected receivables for the individual projects to arrive at the total projected work in place for the entire department. It is, then, the financial counterpart to multiproject scheduling, as discussed in Section 2. It will become the graphic display of current status of the company's operations, and the summary of the short range total production outlook and its relation to the organization's known capacity. In some instances, then, it may also become a measure of organizational efficiency.

In the discussion that follows, the short procedure for constructing the Maxi-MOST integration will be developed. Examples will be included to illustrate the technique completely, and many of the possible uses and advantages of the integration and its status line will be explored. Although several interesting and effective uses will be outlined, this chapter should not be assumed to be exhaustive of all possible uses of the procedure and its results, but rather as the open door to many more advantages to be gained. This, as you'll see, will be limited only by the user's imagination and resources as the system is used and becomes a familiar part of planning.

Procedure

Earlier in this section, the techniques for assembling and assigning dollar amounts to scheduled activities, projecting the data, recording the status information, and using the results have been detailed. These processes will have been completed by the managers and staff who have been charged with the responsibility for the individual project's success. The data required for this procedure, then, has to this point already been accurately and completely produced.

The first step therefore in the construction of the Maxi-MOST integration is assembling the information from each individual project. This involves securing from each project throughout the organization or department the projected receivable curves, including the tabulation of the pertinent data as illustrated in Figures 8-8 and 8-9, together with all status line analyses available to this point.

To construct the Maxi-MOST integration, simply add up the

MOST FINANCIAL PLANNING 157

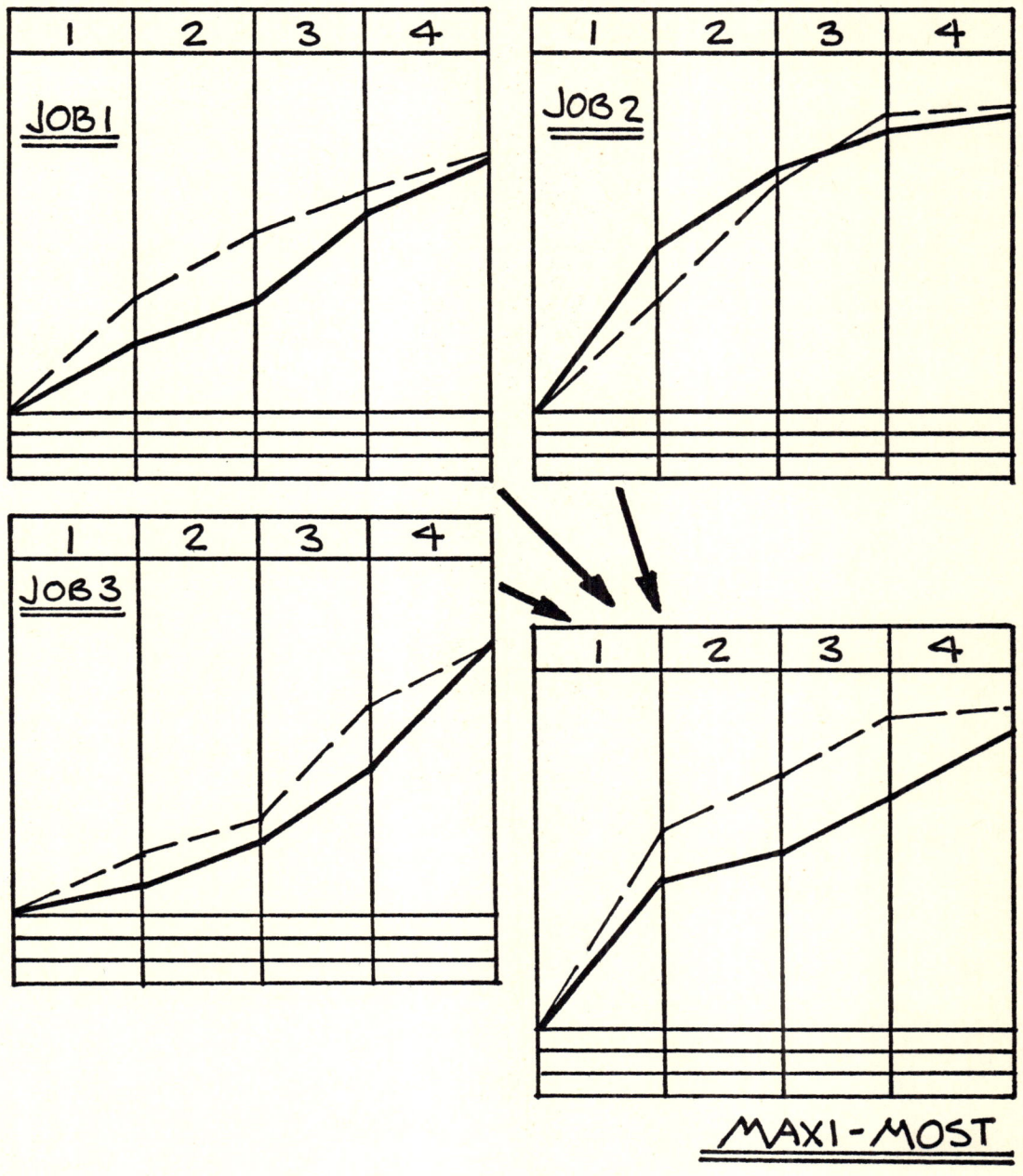

THE MAXI-MOST INTEGRATION

Figure 8-12

projected receivables for the respective periods of each project to arrive at the total projected receivables for the organization as of the date of the projection. This is demonstrated in Figure 8-12.

It is important to include with each Maxi-MOST integration the date of the integration, the specific projects included in the analysis, and summaries highlighting those projects and the appropriate explanations for exceptionally good or exceptionally poor performance. A thorough summary will also include brief descriptions to management of any get-well plans that have been or will be implemented, and a general statement of the overall organization completion of the total performance of the production department.

THE STATUS INDEX

At this point, for the Maxi-MOST integration, or previously for the individual projects, the general performance summary to management should include a status index (detailed in Chapter 7) which will represent by a single number the performance of the department relative to the projected performance. To a degree, the index will define the ability of the company to accomplish the production goals that it has set before itself, notwithstanding its abilities to plan, operate, and control, and the effectiveness at solving problems and overcoming setbacks.

The index, then, is nearly synonymous with percentage of completion. It is simply the percentage of the actual completion (status) of work in place in relation to the projected work for a given period. Because, as we have seen, each period represents a cumulative amount, the index will average-in the performance of the previous periods.

To calculate the index, divide the planned requisition amount by the actual requisition amount, and multiply this by the actual progress divided by the planned progress:

$$\frac{\text{Planned Requisition Amount}}{\text{Actual Requisition Amount}} \times \frac{\text{Actual Progress}}{\text{Planned Progress}} = \text{Status Index}$$

Refer back to Chapter 7 (Work Performance) for detailed examples.

It should be clear that an index number below 1.0 indicates a loss of production or some other problem that requires management attention and correction. A 1.0 will show that performance is exactly what has been cumulatively projected for the period. It is a cue that the project is currently in an acceptable state, but the

MOST FINANCIAL PLANNING 159

status may be fragile, and the continued acceptable performance by all parties is critical to the maintainance of the "acceptable" status. It is obvious now that an index number above 1.0 will highlight a performance of the department (or of particular individuals if a single project is being reviewed) that is that much above and beyond what had been set down and distributed as the written objectives of the individual projects and/or of the department as a whole. As noted before in the discussion of the status line analysis, this information must not be taken as an absolute indication. Instead, it must be considered relative to the indices of past periods and those results at least roughly extrapolated into the future periods, before confidence can realistically be placed in the knowledge of the project's or department's exceptional performance.

The Maxi-MOST is now complete. The answers to many of the same questions that were outlined for the status line analysis will also be valuable here. Their significance expands from the impact of a single project to that of the entire department or organization. In addition, the uses of the Maxi-MOST might expand to include further analysis and development that may identify important concepts such as:

1. The impact of significant claims, litigation, or arbitration on the entire organization; the comparison of the short range winning litigation with the long range impact of court costs.

2. Manpower loading and total projected payroll.

3. The consolidation of procurement for items common to several projects (whether or not the organization's purchasing function is centralized).

4. Exceptionally good or poor performance on the part of a subcontractor or supplier that is carrying over to other projects, and exhibiting a significant effect on the total performance (status index).

5. Delays in owner payments that are requiring excessive borrowing to finance operations.

6. Unjustified or unsupported reasons for owner delays in final payments or release of retainage amounts.

In summary, the important thing is to maintain the awareness that, in spite of the simplicity of the procedure, and although many of the uses of the status line analysis, Maxi-MOST integration, and the status index have been described and correlated with each other here, the maximum effectiveness of the procedure is yet to be achieved. As always, the possibilities are limited only by the needs and the creativeness of the users.

FOUR

Leadership Development for Personal and Professional Gain

9
The MOST Effective Project Leader

LEADERSHIP

Project leadership (or project management) is a general management activity encompassing planning, control, supervision, and the engineering or manufacturing involved in producing an end item, study, or whatever. It is basically getting work done through people with very specific objectives which, when achieved, mean the end of the project manager's function. The project manager usually has no line authority over organizations producing the items which must be delivered or completed. Communications must therefore be very clear, prompt, and comprehensive, and frequently cut across intercompany and intracompany lines.

With the limited life span of a project, the very difficult problems involved, and the potential glare of unfavorable criticism, why would anyone want to be a project leader? For one reason only — because it is one of the best jobs in the world! In terms of broad responsibility, esprit, contribution to the company, and sense of accomplishment, few other industrial activities can compare with it. The increasing demand for good project leaders indicates that they will called upon for their talents in increasing numbers. Good project leaders are also important for the company's reputation because they are entrusted with the mission of producing satisfactory results within the time and cost contemplated.

The increasing demand for highly skilled project leaders must be met from an age group which is already in short supply due to the slowed birth rate during the past few years. Hopefully, this book will help to bridge the gap between the requirement for and the availability of capable project management personnel.

THE PROJECT LEADER

Project leadership consists of overall management of the project to insure that proper management reporting is maintained and that the other tasks are properly coordinated to maintain design and performance requirements; all within approved costs and schedules. The purpose of a project leader is to insure achievement of these objectives through functional organization and over their special interests. The project leader's role is basically one of planning, operating, directing, controlling, and motivating the project team.

The project leader has authority only for project direction over the organizations producing the end items and their support and administrative organizations. Herein lies one of the project leader's biggest problems: how to get the utmost in project effort when the people are responsible to someone else for pay raises, promotion, performance, and other aspects of line relationship.

The leader is right at the focal point of the major problem areas. How he or she handles them has a direct bearing on whether the project is successful, partially successful, or cancelled. The areas the leader is most concerned with are: project planning, project control, fiscal and cost control, profit, customer relations, stop work, and anything that may be required beyond the contract.

BACKGROUND OF THE PROJECT LEADER

An effective project leader is an individual who combines personal qualities, skills, and knowledge in a unique way to bring about the successful completion of a program. Some will argue that effective leaders are a unique breed who come to the force because their own intrinsic qualities and no amount of training will make it happen. Others will say that only the knowledge can be taught. Still others will say that meaningful experience is the only way to bring about the development. Since there is an element of truth in each of these viewpoints, we believe that we should push ahead toward the first milestone; identification of the specific knowledge and skills that we feel project leaders should possess. Identifying the personal qualities required might also be worthwhile to help in selecting the right candidates for development.

Knowledge Required

1. Technical competence in the product or technology area in which they operate.

2. Complete understanding of what the program is contractually obligated to do. This requires an understanding of the Statement of Work, all contractual provisions, the applicable MIL Specs, and any other qualifying documents. This is critical since it gives the leader the basic ingredients for the Program Plan, a sense of direction, and the ability to recognize changes in scope.

THE MOST EFFECTIVE PROJECT LEADER

3. Understanding of planning, scheduling, and control techniques.

4. Understanding of how the company functions, particularly the organizations that will have a significant impact on the success of the program. The leaders must understand how the program will interface with operations, product assurance, and technical documentation, and be familiar with the associated paperwork.

5. Understanding of how to structure and staff their organization. This requires that they know the manpower and resources available.

6. Understanding of Program Reporting.

    Report requirements - technical and cost.
    Internal reporting requirements.

    These are particularly important since they impact on the credibility that project leaders will engender with their customers and with internal management.

7. Understanding of purchasing/subcontracting procedures since they can seriously impact on performance.

8. Understanding of applicable security regulations.

Skills Required

1. Ability to size up resources and to effectively bargain for the resources, manpower, and facility essential to the success of the program.

2. Ability to communicate effectively with program team members, internal management, and customers.

3. Ability to properly and adequately delegate work to team members to clearly define their roles, their scopes, their outputs, and (in short) all of their responsibilities.

4. Ability to work with people to engender team spirit and a high level of output from a diverse group of specialists on the Program Team as well as in supporting organizations.

5. Ability to anticipate or identify technical, schedule, cost, or contractual problems. The ability to develop solutions or appropriate "work arounds."

6. Ability to identify and negotiate change orders in scope in order to add-to rather than dissipate program resources.

Personal Qualities Required.

Personal qualities are pretty much innate and ingrained and cannot be changed to any great extent after early stages of childhood. They are mentioned here not as a subject for development, but to help identify candidates who will have the greatest chance of benefiting from the development program.

1. Confidence in self and in the ability to lead the program team.

2. Boundless energy, stamina, and resiliency.

3. Aggressiveness in pursuing goals, yet disposed to conciliation rather than confrontation.

4. Complete integrity in dealing with subordinates, contributing organizations, internal management, and customers.

5. Sound judgement.

Normally, the project leaders and their staffs are selected from functional areas within the company or from other projects which are phasing down. Upon completion of the project, they return to functional organizations until new projects come along.

By training, experience, or both, project leaders are usually proficient in scheduling and budget techniques, general planning, and getting things done through people; and they understand marketing, contracting, and control, as well as the technology involved. They know and understand the contract thoroughly, sustain the company's interest in the objectives of the project, and maintain the ability to communicate with the people working toward these objectives.

PLANNING CYCLE

The purpose of planning, as was once said, "is not to show how precisely we can predict the future, but rather to uncover the things we must do today in order to have a future."

No other aspect of project leadership is so essential to success as planning. Most of the troubles that confront project management on the rocky road to completion of the project are traceable to faulty planning - whether it be unrealistic, incomplete, or too broad - or just plain lack of plans.

The human animal has a natural aversion to planning, perhaps because most of us feel confident of meeting a problem when we come to it, or perhaps because trying to translate possible eventualities into concrete actions is such a difficult mental process, particularly when the need for the action may never arise. The incentive to planning is, therefore, difficult to come by.

Probably the most effective incentive to planning is experience. The individual who has experienced a project running out of control, or who has been faced with the impact of a sudden change, can appreciate the need for planning better than a person who has not. This person becomes a believer in planning because of the awareness that poor planning can lead to:

1. Loss of control due to ineffective budgeting.

2. Loss of control due to unrealistic scheduling.

3. Loss of control by not organizing for effective action.

4. Loss of control over subcontracts.

5. Loss of profit by too-low estimates, incurring undue risks and insufficient preparation for negotiations.

6. Loss of morale and incentive on the part of project personnel, resulting in overruns and delinquent deliveries.

7. Loss of confidence by the customer.

8. Loss of contract.

Planning starts in the proposal stage, when the proposal team interprets the customer's requirements in terms of specific definitive tasks and determines the general means of accomplishing these tasks. Proposal managers (who often become project leaders) and their teams determine the organization structure, schedules, manpower requirements, in-house and subcontract efforts, facilities requirements, and other aspects of how they would go about the job if awarded the contract. If their proposal is the successful one, the teams usually improve the plan and go into greater detail during negotiations, since the customer ordinarily expects the project team to be off and running as soon as the notice of award is transmitted. The initial operations plan is the keystone on which the project's success or failure is based.

Planning is a continuous function, however. As the project progresses and foresight sharpens with the passage of time, the mole hills of previous perspectives become the mountains of the immediate future. Changes in depth and scope of planning are inevitable. For these reasons, project leadership will find it necessary to review and update project plans frequently, and to build flexibility into their plans.

Planning can certainly be overdone. Planning to a depth beyond that in which pertinent information can be obtained is impractical. Planning to a depth for which pertinent information can be obtained but to which action is rarely or never directed is impractical at best and irresponsible at worst.

For the leader's purposes, planning two levels down, to the subtask level, is probably sufficient for control. Task and subtask managers will normally need more detailed plans, that is, plans two levels down from their plane of responsibility. However, the practical depth will be determined by the answers to such questions as:

1. What efforts are critical to the success of the project?

2. What levels have an administrator assigned to the planning and control function?

3. What efforts extend over a significant period of the contract?

4. Which efforts involve significant expenditures?

Specific planning to a great depth leads to a feeling of "let's stop this paper mill and get to work." The operation and other plans may thereby be undermined and become sterile by being considered as merely a paper exercise. The scope of planning will vary, naturally, with the extent and scope of the project. A small, single-function project, such as a study, requires a relatively simple plan. A large, complex, multifunction project may require one or more volumes to provide adequate attention and direction. All projects worthy of the name, however, whatever the length and scope, should have a written plan covering what is going to be done, how, when, by whom, for how many dollars, what the major foreseeable problems are, and how they will be overcome. This documented plan is not so much for the leader's own use as it is a means of <u>communicating</u> the basis for project operations to others. It also serves as a reference for project leadership to determine whether, as work progresses, intermediate goals may have to be changed, or schedules slipped, or an overrun may be developing which might not otherwise be detected without a written reference.

"You can't schedule thought processes," some managers of study projects like to say. Actually, the study project leader does plan the project approach when mentally figuring how much time can be allowed for planning and manning the project for study and discussion and for preparation and processing the final report. A reluctance to admit that one is actually planning is really a reluctance to put down on paper what is being done anyway. Just as no project has unlimited funds or time to completion, so must all projects be planned in order to stay within those parameters.

The extent to which planning tasks apply to each of these plans differs according to the nature, duration, and scope of the project. The extent may change, too, during the life of the project. The project leader may want to make a periodic review of project planning, perhaps prior to a quarterly review or other pause in normal project operations, in order to review the need for adding or eliminating planning tasks, for each type of plan. A review should occasionally be made of even the basic project structure, such as task breakdown and reporting structure, to keep plans significant and alive.

The initial breakdown divides contractually deliverable items into logical tasks, according to the function of the item (hardware, report, service, or operation, the skills required) and to the geographical or other logical basis for dividing work. This task breakdown sets the stage for all subseqent planning. Changes in this breakdown, therefore, have a multiplier effect, and should be avoided by careful and thorough analysis. It may develop, however, that a subtask is of primary, rather than secondary, importance, and should be a task in itself; or a task may, on further definition, turn out to be a routine function which can be grouped with one or more subtasks and be better relegated to subtask status. If the advantages in project control warrant, changes of this type should be made, taking into consideration the pros and cons involved.

ATTRIBUTES AND FAILURES OF LEADERSHIP

During the past twenty-five years, some of the experts on leadership have collaborated in extensive research and study, compared findings, and conducted many classroom seminars to share their findings. They have also reviewed techniques developed in Japan, Germany, England, and other countries, and have discovered many of their findings to be the same. In their final analysis, they have compiled a list of approximately 300 attributes of good leadership. From this, the experts tailored down their list to the top eleven, and prioritized these in order of importance (Figure 9-1).

Listed as number five is "Definiteness of Plans." This indicates that good leadership depends upon good planning ability and rates it high on the list of attributes. Of course, to be efficient in planning, one should have a working knowledge of successful planning techniques and gain sufficient experience to be an asset to the success of the planning profession.

On the other hand, Figure 9-2 lists the top ten prioritized causes of failure in leadership from the above experts' findings of over 250 listings. "Inability to Organize Details (plan)" is number <u>one</u>. This indicates that poor planning, lack of or inabililty to use proper tools or techniques is the major cause of failure. There is evidence that this is one of the major reasons for companies or businesses, large or small, closing their doors.

THE MAJOR ATTRIBUTES OF LEADERSHIP

1. UNWAVERING COURAGE

2. SELF CONTROL

3. A KEEN SENSE OF JUSTICE

4. DEFINITENESS OF DECISION

5. <u>DEFINITENESS</u> <u>OF</u> <u>PLANS</u>

6. THE HABIT OF DOING MORE THAN PAID FOR

7. A PLEASING PERSONALITY

8. EMPATHY AND UNDERSTANDING

9. MASTERY OF DETAIL

10. WILLINGNESS TO ASSUME FULL RESPONSIBILITY

11. COOPERATION

Figure 9-1

THE TEN MAJOR CAUSES OF FAILURE IN LEADERSHIP

1. <u>INABILITY</u> <u>TO</u> <u>ORGANIZE</u> <u>DETAILS</u> <u>(PLAN)</u>
2. UNWILLINGNESS TO RENDER HUMBLE SERVICE
3. EXPECTATION OF PAY FOR WHAT THEY "KNOW" INSTEAD OF WHAT THEY DO WITH THAT WHICH THEY KNOW
4. FEAR OF COMPETITION FROM FOLLOWERS
5. LACK OF IMAGINATION
6. SELFISHNESS
7. INTEMPERENCE
8. DISLOYALTY
9. EMPHASIS ON THE "AUTHORITY" OF LEADERSHIP
10. EMPHASIS ON TITLE

Figure 9-2

Much has been written on the subject of leadership in recent years and we want to emphasize the importance of good leadership as part of one's success in reaching the goals for the future. Hopefully, with experience gained by the use of some of the techniques outlined in this book, a planner will never abdicate his or her leadership responsibility and fall victim to #1 on Figure 9-2.

10
Controlling Project Administration for Successful Completion and Profit

MAKE OR BUY

This decision is generally made according to company policy, usually by a board established for this purpose, and, in certain contracts, in accordance with the customer's wishes. Changes in the project which result in expanding or reducing the effort, or particicularly good or bad subcontractor performance, may indicate the advisability of changing the initial decision. It is, however, an unusually fortunate project leader who can influence a decision to switch from the original plan. Once the initial decision has been made (perhaps against the leader's wishes) the project leader is usually stuck with the in-house organization or subcontractor selected.

PROJECT SUMMARY

A project planning summary or some kind of document outlining applicable plans and planning tasks is an essential tool of project leadership. It provides guidance in developing the documented plans which form the basis for project operations (see Figure 10-1 on the next page).

In reviewing planning for weaknesses, the project leader needs to analyze planning tasks for their effect on each other, from both project and functional viewpoints. (The same facility may be required by two subtasks at the same time, for instance.) Total manpower, rates of expenditure, and schedules must be in accordance with contract authorizations and requirements.

Planning, even to the most experienced project team, is not an easy job, but it is made easier by the knowledge that sound, thorough planning will help avoid most of the pitfalls which befall a project. Most of the incidents noted in this book have some bearing on planning or lack of plans. Perhaps others' experiences will help

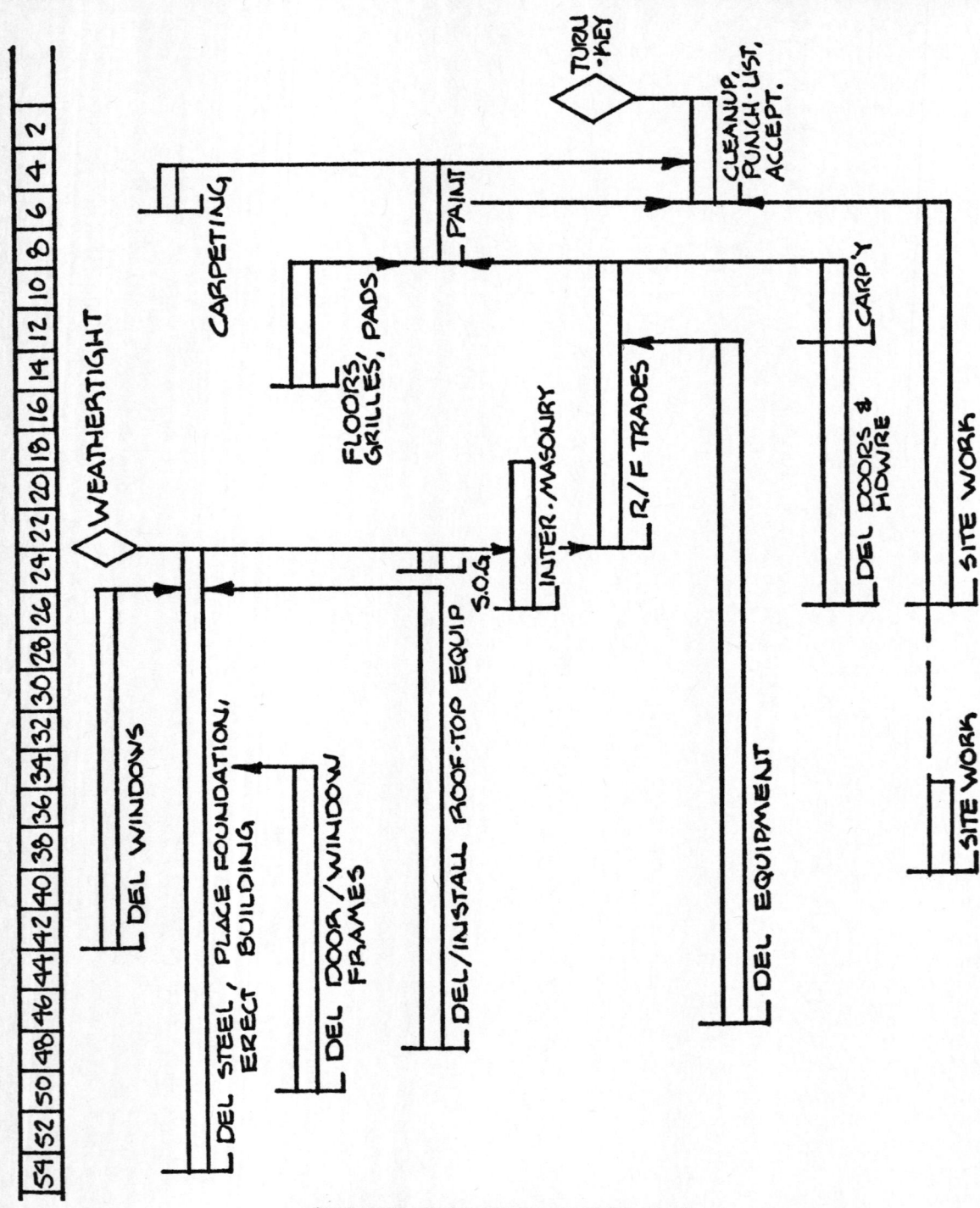

SUMMARY PLAN FROM FIGURE 2-8

Figure 10-1

CONTROLLING PROJECT ADMINISTRATION
175

illustrate the importance of project planning.

Little has been said in this section on planning for technical performance and reliability. Planning these activities is part of the project leader's normal sphere of responsibility, although actual planning may be developed by the functional area concerned. The project leader must be thoroughly familiar with these plans and understand their effect on administrative planning; otherwise project planning is likely to become after-the-fact.

A reminder of the basic principle of general administration: in order to be carried out effectively, the manager of the organization which is to perform a task must be a real contributor to the plan. Not only will more effective action result but the plan will also be a better one.

And lastly, the planning definition that applies in this book:

Planning is to put into writing a list of jobs, tasks, or activities to do something or make something, put their parts in their proper order, show their interdependencies and interrelationships, estimate the duration or elapse time for each function, and eventually, by summing these items, estimate the amount of time to complete all tasks.

THE TEAM

The term "Team" has been mentioned many times, and now we shall elaborate on the need for it.

For any plan to be valid, it must be, in its final form, the result of a team effort with all interested departments and activities represented on the team constructing the plan. This is particularly true in the case of CPM/MOST networks and schedules because of the necessity for agreement among the departments of the interactions which are an essential part of the plan. Among other reasons for the necessity of the team approach is the fact that the networks must represent the total project task, inherent in which are the requirements of each department or work area within the organization, generally known in detail only by the respective members of each organization. The individual representatives as members of the team are most likely to remain interested in keeping a plan updated in which they personally had an important part of construction. Also, since the MOST schedule will be derived from this plan, the persons who must meet the schedule will know that they helped to establish it, and thus provide the basis for positive management action inasmuch as their part in this work will have been sanctioned by the department heads. And, finally, the realization that data will be fed back to the personnel who provided the input to the plan and schedule will result in more interest and commensurate accuracy of input information to the technique.

Team members may come from departments such as Project Engineering, Purchasing, Subcontractors, Architects, Accounting, Quality Control, and whatever other departments may be involved. Because planning and scheduling cut across department lines, a planner may be selected to assist the team in collecting, organizing, and coordinating information. The planner will assemble input data, compute schedules, and apply these data to the plan.

The team supplies the planner with information about the jobs of a project. To arrange the jobs in their proper sequence and to determine their interrelationships, the planner lists all jobs with the following key questions in mind:

* What job or jobs must be completed first?

* What job or jobs can be done at the same time?

* What job or jobs cannot start until other jobs are completed?

Sooner or later, as the project heads into its final stages, the leader realizes that the team should begin to phase down, consistent with the contract and practical requirements. The leader can do this in either a crude or considerate way. The leader's successes in getting these people to work on future projects or activities may depend upon how they are released from the project. He or she can help them find desirable openings in the company, in conjunction with the personnel manager, and release them as openings occur; or the leader can in effect tell them "We don't need you any more. Find yourself another assignment." A very capable administrative manager on an electronic intelligence project, for instance, who got the latter treatment is not likely to seek a project assignment again. The leader has a responsibility to project people to "look after the troops" by maintaining the desirability of being on the project team. Their experience will go a long way toward the success of a future project.

SUMMARY

The actual benefits realized through the use of MOST have been varied and far reaching. This new system has had wide acclaim by the government, construction, and industry alike. When the concept is understood and used in the manner for which it was designed, any savings which result in a single better-scheduled project, or the achievement of the desired objective event significantly ahead of schedule, will pay for the effort expended on MOST many times over.

MOST, like any good management technique, should provide a capability which cannot be attained by other methods; it should be economical to operate, and dynamic enough to provide the necessary data for management when needed; and above all, it should serve management and not have management serve MOST. Therefore, careful examination should be made before any advanced planning or applied program is implemented. We're confident that when such a careful examination is completed, MOST will be selected for your across-the-board planning and scheduling system. MOST will provide a needed, easy to implement capability that other techniques will not provide.

The simplicity and clarity of a MOST schedule allows for evaluating manpower, resources, and jobs readily; identifying weak spots and potential trouble areas rapidly, and pinpointing long lead jobs easily. Also, a MOST schedule offers well-organized data that permits fast, reliable, and comprehensive reporting. Because MOST schedules are simple and relatively small, they reduce the drafting time and reproduction costs. Then, too, personnel can learn the system in a brief time. Since relatively few people are required to set up the MOST function and to provide efficient monitoring of programs, the system adds little to project costs (The system will definitely reduce project costs if applied against a CPM budget). Companies using MOST will find it indispensable now and in the future as a powerful management scheduling tool.

In the construction business, MOST has been the answer many have been looking for. Small and large firms are looking for a compliment or a substitute for CPM - one that is not only economical, but faster to implement, easier to evaluate, and above all, with quicker "visibility" for construction management to make proper decisions. MOST was introduced to construction in 1964, and has been found to be superior with or without CPM. Although CPM is being taught to firms that would like to continue using CPM, at least for the planning phase, in due time MOST has or will become their scheduling way of life. Many have switched not only for its superior visibility, but because it can be so easily implemented and used for weekly tracking and reporting without a computer.

In construction, we believe that once the bid is accepted, it is the scheduling thereafter that becomes the principal all-encompassing function. Many books on CPM, PERT, and others devote more time to planning and forget that it is scheduling in construction that is the more important. As mentioned earlier, this book alleviates all of the philosophy and unnecessary verbiage that may confuse the reader and hinder complete understanding of the material. MOST is simplicity in scheduling. Contrary to techniques such as CPM, this book is all you will need to use MOST to get the _most_ out of each project.

APPENDIX

CPM (Critical Path Method) Scheduling

This appendix is not intended to teach the fine points of CPM, because many books have been written on the subject.

This appendix will cover the basics and will review the simplification of CPM. As mentioned earlier, CPM will be used as a planning technique, and when CPM is used, MOST will pick the project up from there as the superior method to reflect the true indication of the project's progress through its dynamic visibility.

WHAT IS CRITICAL PATH METHOD (CPM)?

CPM is one of the most powerful, most discussed, and least understood of management planning and control techniques. It has been extensively applied to development efforts in aerospace, defense, commercial, and construction activities and industries.

CPM's usefulness as a management tool for small and simple projects has been largely overshadowed because of its initial application to large and complex construction projects. CPM has been effective for efforts across a broad range of projects in size and complexity. It has proven its value as a management planning tool for projects ranging from the production of Broadway plays to the construction of dams, to the development of the vastly complex Polaris Weapon System.

Three things are required to apply CPM effectively on a project: first, the fundamentals of CPM (including the network and time estimating) must be mastered. Secondly, CPM must be applied

intelligently to each project in full acknowledgment of the
managerial requirements, the complexity of the problem, and the cost
and time in implementation. Third, although CPM networks can be
generated manually, effective and practical use on any project
requires a computer.

CPM is a computer technique for defining and integrating
activities and events which must be accomplished on a timely basis to
assure coordinated completion of project objectives. It defines
areas of effort whereby trade-offs in time, resources, or performance
will enable management to meet scheduled dates. As any management
tool, it is there to provide information and to assist decision
makers. It does not make the decisions for them. It is designed to
assist managers in estimating, budgeting, and controlling the
schedule and technical performance required to achieve project
objectives by providing:

* A clear definition of the project objectives.

* A plan of the work to be performed.

* Good communications among project personnel and the various
  levels of project management.

* Knowledge of current project status.

* Accurate estimates of time to complete the project.

* Reliable monitoring of elements involving technical uncertainty
  and risk.

* Early identification of potential schedule improvements or
  slippages.

CPM is most useful in one-of-a-kind or few-of-a-kind projects,
such as engineering development or building construction (as opposed
to high volume production programs). Its most significant advantages
as a planning technique lie in its ability to simulate the effect of
alternate decisions or planning sequences under consideration to
study their effect upon the project deadlines, prior to actual
implementation, and to forecast the probability of successfully
meeting those deadlines.

The three factors that influence progress in executing a project
using CPM are time, resources, and technical performance. Time is
the variable that can be used as a common denominator to reflect
planned resource application and performance specifications.

APPENDIX

DEFINITIONS AND SYMBOLS

Before CPM can be discussed, some important definitions are required:

1. CPM Network

The CPM network is a graphic description of the plan, showing the sequential steps needed to reach a stated objective. It depicts events and jobs and their interrelationships, and recognizes the progress that must be made in one task before subsequent tasks can begin. The network must be comprehensive and must include all significant interdependencies and interactions required to perform the project.

In other words, the network is a flow chart with events similar to milestones and jobs. Thus, the CPM network becomes only a slightly different means of showing the "Christmas Tree" type of planning used quite widely (the Bar Chart, in any event, is still probably the most widely used scheduling method in construction today).

2. Activities (or Jobs)

Activities, or jobs, are the work efforts of a project. They represent the action of the network, such as preparing, designing, building, testing, negotiating, developing, and analyzing. Jobs are the time-consuming elements, the employment of human effort, facilities, or materials, over which the manager must have control.

A job in a CPM network is represented by an arrow which links two or more successive events.

3. Event

In CPM, an "event" is a specific, definable accomplishment in a project plan, recognizable at a particular instant in time. An event does not consume time or resources and is shown on a network as a square, circle, or other geometric design. In short, an event is the start or completion of an activity, not the actual performance of the activity. Therefore, all tasks, jobs, or activities must begin with an event and end with an event.

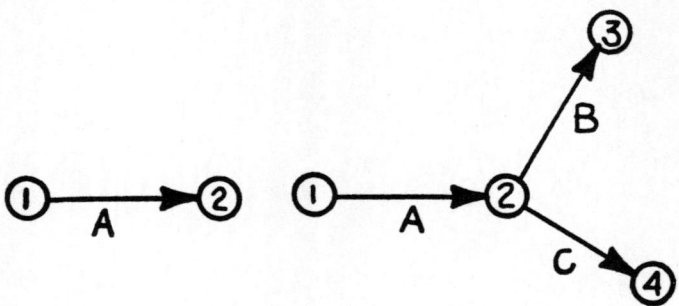

4. Constraints

The term "constraint" is used to indicate the relationship of an event to a succeeding job wherein the job may not start until the event preceding it has occurred, and the relationship of a job to a succeeding event wherein the event cannot occur until all jobs preceding it have been completed.

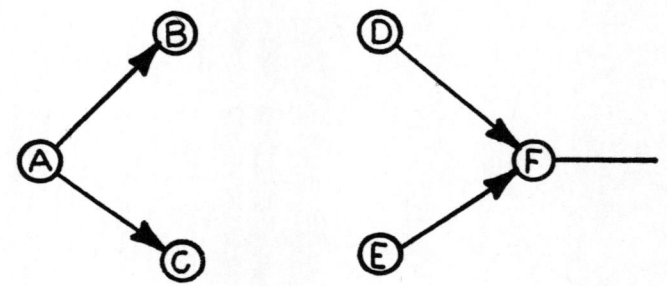

A CONSTRAINS B·C   D·E CONSTRAINS F

5. Time Estimating

Time estimating is determining the time required to perform each job in the network. The estimate is based on:

a. Customary levels of manpower and other resource availability.

b. Normal resource application rates or work schedules (40 hours per week, the normal number of shifts, etc.).

That is, the time estimate is determined by calculating how long

APPENDIX

it would take to complete a job under typical local working conditions.

6. Planning

Planning is determining what jobs are involved in a given project, their logical sequence, and their interrelationships. A plan should follow a uniform system which is understood by all.

7. Scheduling

Scheduling is giving the plan a timetable; relating it to the calendar.

8. Critical Path

The critical path in a CPM network is the particular sequence or sequences of jobs (from the start event) that has the greatest negative (or least positive) path float (i.e., consumes the longest time in reaching the end event). If an activity along the critical path is affected, the completion date of the project is correspondingly affected (hence the word "critical"). There is no room along this path for error without affecting the end date.

9. Dummy Event and Job

Only one job can originate and culminate in any given pair of start and end events. If two or more jobs originate in the same start event and culminate in the same end event, both a fictitious (dummy) event and a fictitious (dummy) job must be introduced to maintain correct logic as far as the computer is concerned.

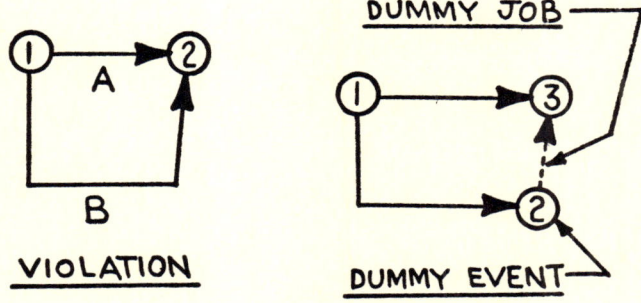

10. Path

Jobs which are related in a series from start to completion.

11. Symbols:

t_e : Expected time (estimated)

T_E : Earliest expected date

T_L : Latest allowable date

Float : $T_L - T_E$

Note that small letters in CPM indicate time, and large letters indicate date.

TIME ESTIMATING – JOBS

With the basic network constructed as in Figure A-1, the common denominator of CPM, time, is applied. The time estimate is to be made in calendar weeks, working days, or whatever span is logical or preferred. Scheduling purists may require calendar weeks and tenths of weeks because they argue that the Gregorian Calendar is the only true common language relative to time, but you and your field superintendent don't normally think in "tenths of weeks," do you?

The basis for time estimates must be made known by the project planning and control function or a team of technical people who can speak for their respective jobs. Generally, this basis will consist of use of the facilities and manpower that are known will exist at the time of accomplishing the job with a single-shift, forty-hour week, at least for the first inputs. As these parameters change, everyone must be informed.

The entire analysis of how the plan can be executed with respect to time depends upon the accuracy of the estimates of expected times for the jobs. Therefore, it is of great importance that these estimates be obtained from the best sources possible. It will be found prudent to obtain the time estimates from departments on an individual basis, in order to insure as nearly as possible an impartial viewpoint, and to eliminate any connotation of scheduling at this stage of planning.

APPENDIX

PLANNING AND SCHEDULING

The difference between a plan and a schedule is made intentionally. The plan represents only the steps that must be accomplished in sequence and shows their interrelationships and interdependencies. The schedule supports the plan by specifying the dates or times on which each job in the plan is to be accomplished to meet the contractually-obligated (scheduled) date of the end item.

An analysis to determine the feasibility of a plan constructed in network form and a schedule to support the plan can be derived by estimating the time necessary to accomplish each job. The first thing to be considered in scheduling any operation is how long each job, activity, or task should take under normal circumstances; i.e., its "normal duration." This is estimated on the basis of previous experience, often in consultation with site superintendent, engineers, subcontractors, or others who are directly connected with the work. If it is a new project which has not been attempted before, the job durations are estimated by a careful analysis of the work to be constructed and the labor available.

NETWORK CONSTRUCTION

Because the network is the basis for the entire CPM system, its construction is treated as a separate subject. The construction of a plan in network form is far from an easy undertaking, but can be completed correctly with careful, systematic application of the network construction rules.

PLANNING RULES

1. The jobs do not represent alternate paths – each line must be traversed to reach the objective of the network.

2. An event cannnot occur until every job preceding it has been completed.

3. A job succeeding an event cannot be started until the event has occurred.

4. An event cannot occur twice – the network loop must not return to an event.

5. Only one job may join any pair of events. Should there actually be two or more jobs between two events, a dummy

activity and event must be added.

6. Every network can have only one beginning and one ending event.

Fundamentally, the CPM technique is based on what is known as the arrow diagram, flow diagram, or network. These diagrams represent the sequence of operations through which a project must be carried from start to completion. Time is the basis upon which the networks are developed.

All jobs take time to accomplish, and for the present, we will assume that any number of people can work on a job (including one). A job is shown on a network as an arrow, and the length of the arrow has no bearing as far as time is concerned.

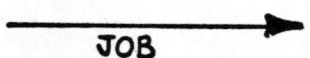

The beginning or end of a job is called an event.

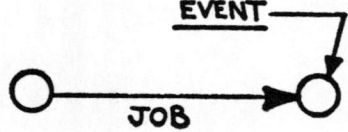

Jobs take time. But the beginning or end of a job is assumed to take no time. That is, they are instantaneous. Since the beginning and end of a job are considered to be instantaneous, the events are therefore instantaneous. Events can be circles, squares, triangles, or whatever configuration the planner wants to use, provided that it remains consistent throughout the network.

There can be more than one job emanating from an event or into an event.

APPENDIX   187

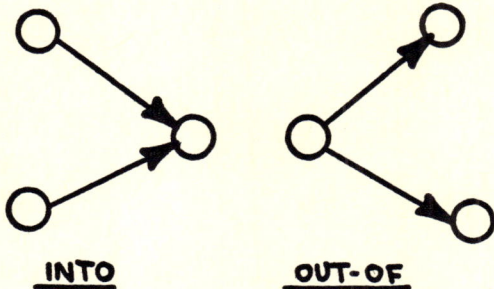

When two or more jobs go into an event, it is referred to as a node point. When two or more jobs emanate from an event, it is called a burst point.

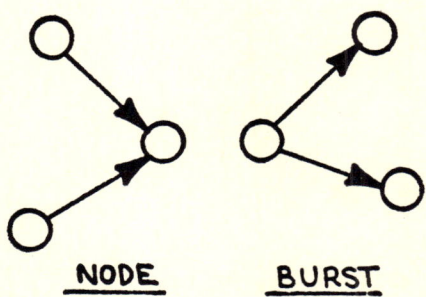

When jobs are related and follow one another in series, this is called a path.

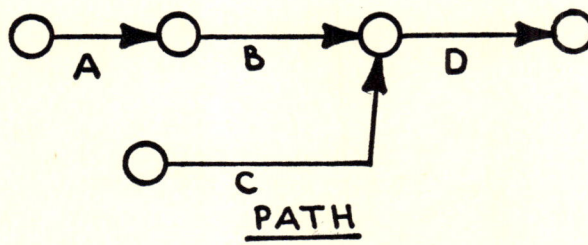

Now let's study a network showing several paths to the end event, Figure A-1:

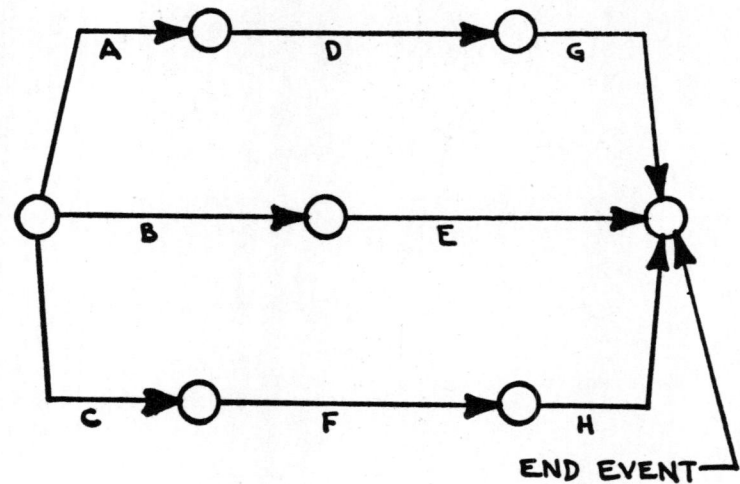

NETWORK OF PATHS

Figure A-1

Jobs A-D-G, and B-E, are different paths, both leading to the end event. Now, in order to complete this network, we must identify the events in order to describe the beginning and ending is by numbering jobs. The most common method of identifying events is by numbering them, making certain that small numbers precede larger numbers.

The major reason for this is for ease in locating specific activities on the diagram while working with the document (many computer programs available today will accept out-of-sequence numbers).

In Figure A-2, the estimated time for job C, between events 1 and 4, is three weeks. This is the Expected Time t_e. The time to complete all of the jobs along the Critical Path, 1-4, 4-6, 6-7, and thus arrive at the end of item H, is the sum of the expected times shown, which is eleven weeks.

APPENDIX

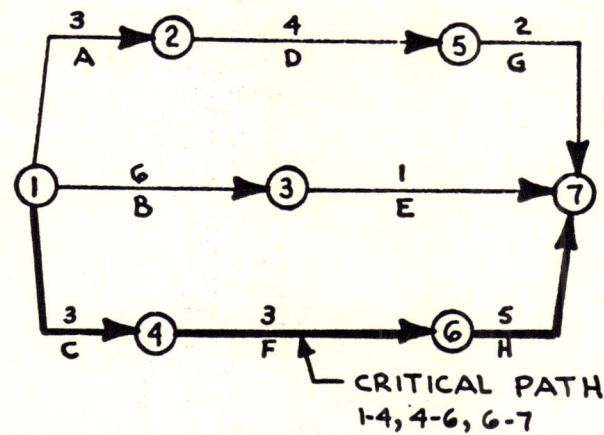

CRITICAL PATH

Figure A-2

Thus, by adding all the jobs along a path, we will arrive at completion dates, known as Expected Date T_E.

The longest path on the network (the one with the most distant T_E) is called the Critical Path, which dictates the schedule.

If the contractual completion date is known, a comparison with the estimated critical path will allow the user to compare the schedule against the contractual date.

The eleven weeks to complete is the earliest possible duration (time to complete) of the project. We have defined the duration for the network, but now we must determine the earliest dates for all events, or the T_E values in a circle above each event.

Figure A-3 illustrates the earliest start dates for all events. Completing this process in sequence from left to right is often referred to as the "Forward Pass."

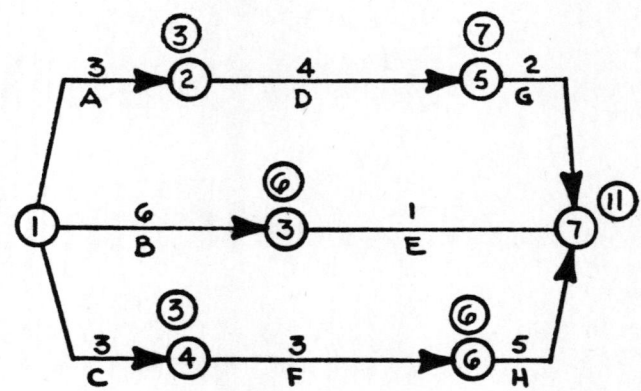

NETWORK OF T_E; THE FORWARD PASS

Figure A-3

The next step is to estimate the latest completion date, T_L, for the end event. The two ways to determine the T_L for the event 7 are: (1) the contractually obligated date, or (2) management decision.

For simplicity, we will assume in the example that both the contractual dates and management decision are the same; 11 weeks to complete. This means the $T_E = T_L$ for the end event.

The critical path in this case must therefore be strictly adhered to, because if any slippage occurs along this path, the schedule will be in jeopardy.

To calculate the T_L for all preceding events, subtract the preceding t_e from the succeeding T_L, as:

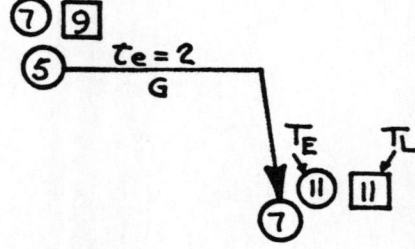

APPENDIX

Performing this process back through the network (from right to left) is referred to as the "Backward Pass."

When all T_L's are calculated, we can now show the amount of float (or slack) time for each job. The float time is the free time or cushion allowed. Float is the difference between the latest and earliest completion dates.

$$F \text{ (Float)} = T_L - T_E$$

Figure A-4 completes the network which can now become a working management tool because the plan is complete, the schedule has been calculated, and float paths are known. For this exercise, we will place the T_L value in a square next to the T_E circles, and the float value in a triangle below the job line.

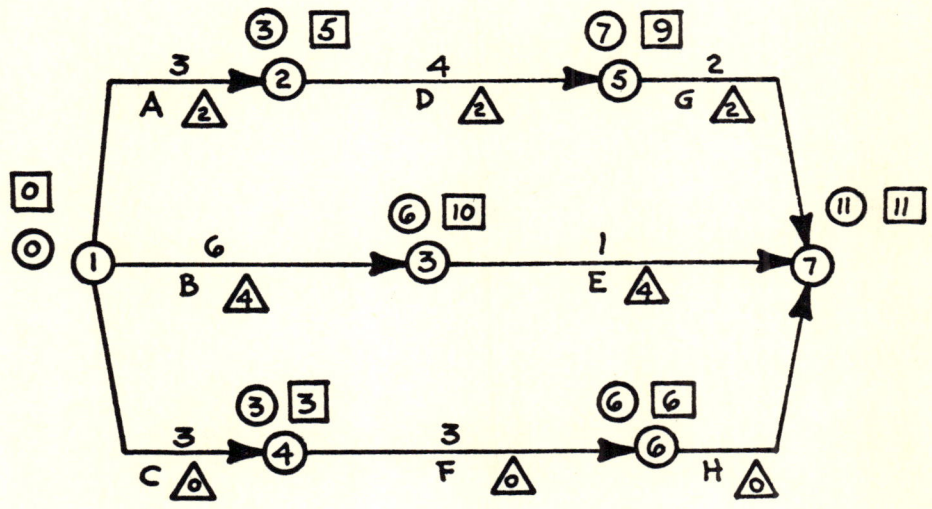

NETWORK COMPLETION

Figure A-4

FLOAT TIME

Each job now shows an expected date and a latest date for completion. If these two dates are compared by subtracting the expected date from the allowed date, the result is a measure of the added time, or cushion, along a path to allow meeting the scheduled date of the objective. The value so derived is known as float. Float may, therefore, be defined as the amount of slippage that can be tolerated along a particular path without adversely affecting the schedule of the objective. Float can be negative and, if so, the amount of slippage that can be tolerated along a particular path is less than zero. In other words, some action must be taken to make time along the path to bring the float back to zero if the scheduled date of the objective is to be met.

Analysis of Figure A-4 indicates that when $T_E = T_L$ for the end event, the float along the critical path will always equal zero. A review of job E, for example, shows that the earliest E can start is 6 weeks and the latest is 10 weeks. This means that E can be delayed 4 weeks, and provided E can be accomplished in one week as shown, the schedule can be met along this path.

The float shown is the allowable float for each job, and must not be included when calculating the time to complete each path. If the early float along a path has been used up, the float down-stream of

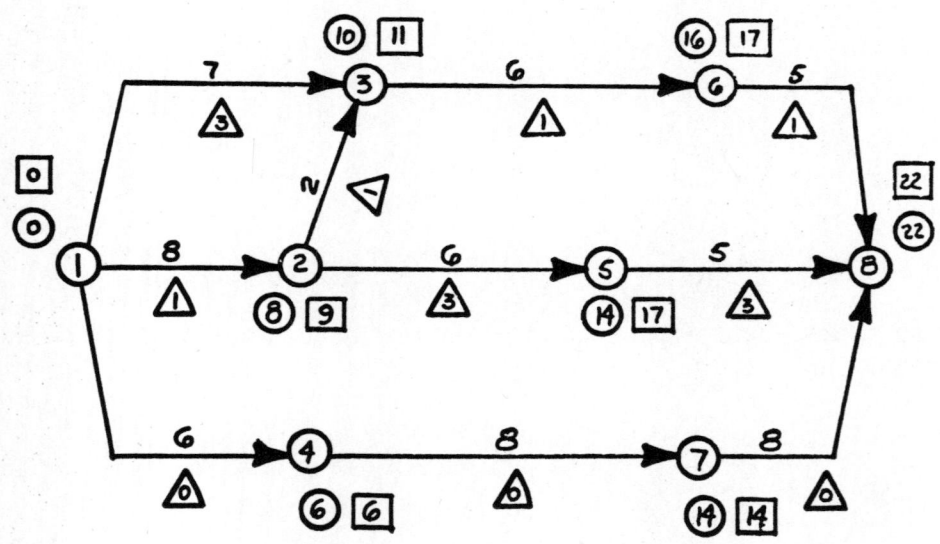

CPM TOTAL CALCULATIONS

Figure A-5

APPENDIX 193

equal value may be used up. A network can show three different float times; namely positive, negative, and zero.

Calculations at both node points and burst points are different from the normal method described. To determine the T_E at a node point, the larger or largest value is used to define the node event. To determine the T_L at a burst point, the smaller or smallest value is used to determine the burst event.

A final calculation rule to remember is that when a job enters a node point anywhere on the CPM plan except the critical path or the last event, the latest date (T_L) for that job is determined by subtracting its t_e from node point T_L.

Figure A-5 illustrates this rule and all of the other calculations necessary for CPM. If one can digest and understand this example, one can do so for any CPM drawn. This figure demonstrates all aspects of a CPM network.

Jobs 1-2, 2-3, and 1-3 are involved in this rule. Note that float for job 1-3 is 3. The normal rule is to subtract 7 from 11 which is 4. The CPM explanation for this change is to proceed beyond the node point as early as possible without affecting the allowable float time for subsequent jobs.

CPM - DOG HOUSE

Now that we have explained the CPM planning technique, let us use the system to plan construction projects, explain rationale, analyze and evaluate.

We will begin with a simple example: the construction of a dog house. Assuming that a father and his son work together, and using inflated times, the plan starts with a list of jobs that must be performed.

DOG HOUSE

		DAYS
1.	Design	6
2.	Shop Drawings	5
3.	Buy Lumber	15
4.	Buy Hardware	10
5.	Build Frame	5
6.	Build Door	3
7.	Shingle Roof	1
8.	Install Hardware	1
9.	Install Door	1
10.	Final Inspection	2

Figure A-6 illustrates the plan which shows that jobs 15-25, 25-35, and 35-40 can be performed by the father. Jobs 15-20, 20-30, and 30-35 can be performed by the son. (This example is converted to MOST in Section 2).

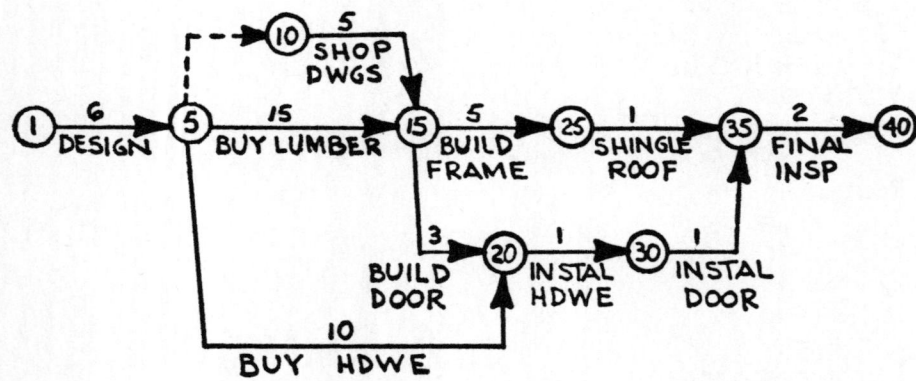

CPM: DOG HOUSE

Figure A-6

APPENDIX

CONSTRUCTION - ONE STORY BUILDING

Now we will proceed with the construction (scheduling) of a small one-story building. This listing and sequence of jobs of the following CPM plan are typical of many construction projects. The flow of jobs and interrelations are similar to large and small projects.

SMALL ONE-STORY BUILDING

		DAYS
1.	Mobilization	5
2.	Footings/Foundation	20
3.	Backfill	5
4.	Steel - Shop Dwgs, Appr., Del.	15, 15, 50
5.	Erect Steel	20
6.	Brick/Block Walls	30
7.	Roofing/Drains	15
8.	Window - Shop Dwgs, Appr., Del.	15, 15, 60
9.	Install Windows, Glass, & Glaze	10
10.	Underground Mech/Elect	5
11.	SOG (Slab on Grade)	5
12.	Metal Studs, Sheet Rock, Tape	20
13.	Rough Mech/Elect	30
14.	Switch Gear - Shop Dwgs, Appr., Del.	20, 15, 80
15.	Mech. Equip. - Shop Dwgs, Appr., Del.	15, 15, 60
16.	Finish Mech/Elect	20
17.	Toilets/Access - Dwgs, Appr., Del.	15, 15, 50
18.	Lighting Fixture - Dwgs, Appr., Del.	10, 15, 60
19.	Carpentry/Millwork	20
20.	Doors - Shop Dwgs, Appr., Del.	10, 15, 40
21.	Painting (Interior)	25
22.	Clean-up	15
23.	Punch List	15
24.	Acceptance	3

Figure A-7 illustrates the plan made from the above list. This plan can include more detail jobs, but this level can be monitored successfully to get the project back on schedule.

The CPM plan, Figure A-7, can be used for any project as a basic flow. Naturally, if a high rise building or multistory business building, shopping center, or any large construction project is to be built, this flow will be expanded. A main objective of construction planning is to weathertight the building. Once the roof is on and the windows installed, we can assume that the building is weathertight. Depending on location, it is generally necessary to

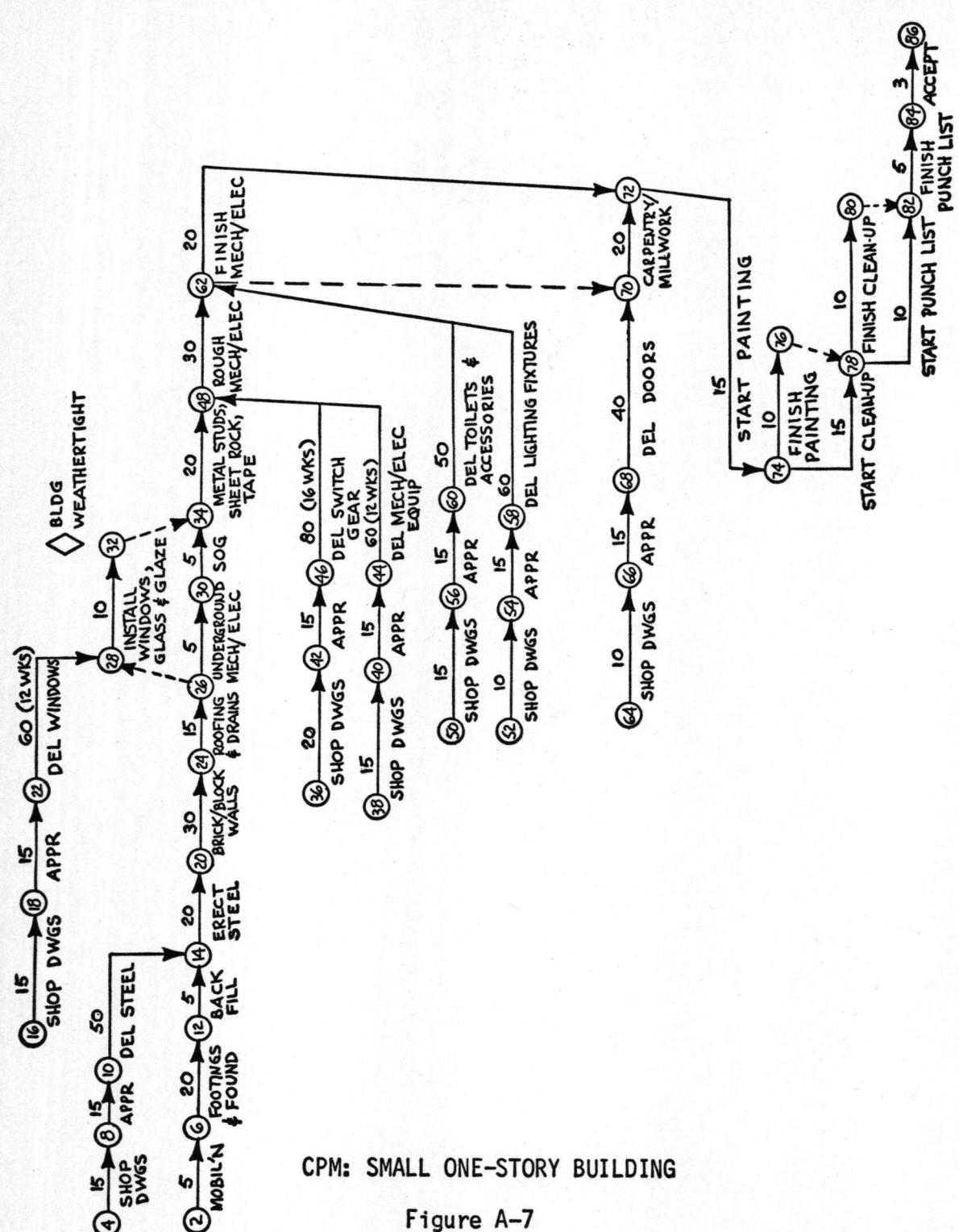

CPM: SMALL ONE-STORY BUILDING

Figure A-7

APPENDIX

plan this weathertight job before the cold sets in. This accommodation will enable many trades to begin interior jobs without interference or down time. (This example, Figure A-7, is converted to MOST in Section 2.)

Index

A

Acknowledgment, Baseline Schedule ..100
Action, Timely 73
Activities - CPM 181, 186
           - MOST 128
Adjusted Schedule 96
Administration, Project 173
Advantages of Proper Notice 98
Agenda, Job Meeting 54
Ahead of Schedule 38
Allotment, Job Estimates 111, 117
Allowable Date, Latest (CPM) 184
Analysis, Schedule 44-47, 65
        , Schedule Report 104
        , Trend 44
Appendix - CPM 179
Arrow Diagram 186
As-Built Schedule 96
As-Planned Schedule 96
Assignment, Change Order Costs 149
          , Cost 132
          , Material Cost 133
Attributes of Leadership 169

B

Background of the Project Leader ...164
Backward Pass 191
Backup Documents 94
Bar Chart 69
         - Limitations 69, 88

Baseline - Cash-Flow Projection 127
         - Release 102
         - Schedule 37, 54
         - Schedule Acknowledgment ..100
         - Schedule Preparation 53
Basic MOST Schedule 31
Behind Schedule 38
Budgeting (MOST/COST)................117
Burst Point 187, 193
Buy, Make or 173

C

Calendar Application 30
Cash-Flow Projection, Baseline 127
Change Order - Costs 149
             - Disproportionate Costs.77
             - Impact 72, 75, 148
             - Lead Times 76
             - Proposals 77
             - Reporting 147
             - Solicitation 77
             - Types 149
Change Orders 69, 71-75
Chart, Bar 69
     , Gantt 69
Claims-Consciousness 87
Commitment, Posting 119
Complete MOST 66
Completion, Percentage of 35
          , Progress 36
Constraint, CPM 182
Contingencies 60

Contract Modification 72
Controlling Manpower 111
Control, Project 53
Cost - Assignment 132
     - Control 117
     - Cumulative 138
     - Individual 138
     - Labor 131
     - Management 111
     - Material 129
     - Total 136, 149
Countdown Schedule 84
CPM 179
    - Activity 186
    - Constraint 182
    - Conversion to MOST 31
    - Definitions 181
    - Expected Date 184
    - Expected Time 184
    - Event 181, 186
    - Network 181, 185
    - Path 184, 187
Critical Path 34, 183, 189
Cumulative - Cost 138
           - Receivable Curve 139
Curve, Problem Area 151
     , Projected Receivables ..137, 139
     , "S" 139
Cycle, Planning 166

D

Definitions - CPM 181
            - Planning 173, 183
            - Scheduling 183
Delay Notes 42, 63, 72, 150
Detail, Level of 55
Diagram, Arrow 186
Disproportionate Change Order Effect.77
Downstream Planning 81
Down Time 61
Dummy Event, Job 183
Duration Application 30

E

Effects, Change Order 77
Estimated - Cash-Flow Projection 127
          - Time (CPM) 182, 184
          - Time (MOST) 31
Estimates, Job 111, 117
         , Material 129
Evaluation, Schedule 44, 46, 65
          , Schedule Report 104
Event - CPM 181, 186
      - Dummy 183, 185
      - Identification 188
Evidence, Requirements for 94
Expected - Date (CPM) 184
         - Time (CPM) 184

F

Failures of Leadership 169
Final - Baseline Release 102
      - Schedule 54, 84
Financial Planning 127
Flags 31
Flat-Lining 152
Float 184, 191
Flow Diagram 186
Forward Pass 190
Free Time 191

G

Gantt Chart 69
Get-Well Plan 42, 60, 63, 69, 86

I

Identification of Events 188
Impact, Change Order 72, 75, 148
Improvements in Performance 97

199

Incentive, Planning 167
Index, Status 123, 158
Individual Cost 138
Integration, Maxi-MOST 156

J

Job Estimates 111, 117
Jobs - CPM 181
     - Dummy 183
Job Meeting Agenda 54

K

Knowledge, Project Leader 164

L

Labor Cost 131
Latest Allowable Date, CPM 184
Leader, Project 163
Leadership 163
           - Attributes 169
           - Failures 169
           - Knowledge 164
           - Qualities 166
           - Skills 165
Lead Times, Change Order 76
Legal Back-up Documents 94
Leveling, Manpower 114
Level of Detail 55
Levels, Planning 168
Level Work 80
Limitations, Bar Chart 69, 88
Line - Flat 152
     - Reporting 29, 38
     - Status 140
Loading - Manpower 112
        - Schedule (Manpower) 111

M

Make or Buy 173
Manpower - Leveling 80, 114
         - Loading 112
         - Loading Schedule 111
         - Management 111
Material - Assignments (Cost) 133
         - Estimates 129
Maxi-MOST Integration 156
Meeting, Job (Agenda) 54
       , Pre-Schedule 53
       , Production 103
Milestones 48, 54
Mini-MOST 67, 94
Modification, Contract 72-75
MOST - Basic Schedule 31
     - Complete 66
     - Conversion to CPM 31
     - /COST 117
     - Financial Planning 127
     - Float 31
     - Mini 67
     - Updating 34, 38
Multiproject Scheduling 80

N

Network - Construction (CPM) 185
        - CPM 181
        - Of T_E 190
Node Point 187, 193
Notes, Delay 42, 63, 72, 150
Notice, Schedule as 98
Notification - Process 99
             - Requirements 74
Numbering Events 188

O

On-Schedule 38
Orders, Change 69, 71-75

P

Pass, Backward 191
    , Forward 190
Path, CPM 184, 189
    , Critical 34, 183, 189
Percentage of Completion 35
Performance, Improvements in 97
          , Work 123
Personal Qualities (Leader) 166
Plan, Get-Well 42, 60
Planning 166
       - CPM 185
       - CPM Rules 185
       - Cycle 166
       - Definition 175, 183
       - Downstream 81
       - Financial 127
       - Incentives 167
       - Levels 168
Plotting Change Orders 147
Point, Burst 187, 193
    , Node 187, 193
Posting Commitment 119
Preliminary Schedule 54
Preparation - Baseline Schedule 53
          - MOST 29
Presentable Evidence, Requirements ..94
Pre-Schedule Meeting 53
Problem-Area Curve 151
Process, Notification 99
Production Meeting 103
Progress - Measuring 124
       - of Completion 36
       - Reporting 42
       - Update 44, 54
Project - Administration 173
       - Control 53
Projected Receivable Tabulation 137
Projection, Baseline Cash-Flow 127
Project Leader 163
          - Background 164
          - Knowledge 165
          - Skills 165
Project Summary 173
Proper Notice 98
Proposals, Change Order 80
Protection of Rights 97

Q

Qualities, Leadership 166

R

Receivables - Projected Tabulation ..137
        - Status Tabulation 144
Release, Final Baseline 102
Reporting - Change Orders 147
       - Line 29, 38
       - Progress 42
       - Status ..39, 40, 45, 86, 140
Report, Schedule Analysis 44, 47, 65
    , Variance 48
Requirements - Evidence 94
         - Notification 74
Rescheduling - MOST 40
Resource Leveling 80
Rights, Protection of 97
Rules, CPM Planning.................185

S

Schedule - Adjusted 96
       - Analysis / Eval. ..44, 46, 65
       - Analysis / Eval. Report ..104
       - As-Built 96
       - as Notice 98
       - As-Planned 96
       - Baseline 37, 54
       - Baseline Acknowledgment ..100
       - Basic MOST 31
       - Behind-On-Ahead 38
       - Countdown 84
       - Definition 183
       - Final 54
       - Multiproject 80
       - Preliminary 54
       - Procedure 54, 58
       - Success-Oriented 60
Scheduling, CPM 185
S-Curve 139
Skills, Project Leader 165
Slack (Float) Time 184, 191

Slippages 91
Solicitation, Change Order 77
Standardization, Size 29
Status – Index 123, 158
       – Line 140
       – Reporting .39, 40, 45, 86, 140
       – Reporting ..39, 40, 45, 86, 140
Success-Oriented Schedule 60
Superintendent Bar Charts 69, 88

T

Tabulation, Projected Receivables ..137
            , Receivable Status 144
Team, the 175
Time, Contingency 60
    , Estimated (CPM) 182, 184
    , Estimated (MOST) 31
    , Expected (CPM) 184
    , Down 61
    , Float, Slack 191
Timely – Action 73
       – Notice 98
Total Cost 136

Tracking 40
Trend Analysis 44
Types, Change order 149

U

Updating – Frequency 34
         – Method 34, 38, 42, 54
         – Progress 44

V

Variance Report 48
Visibility 60, 72, 81

W

Work-Around 42, 63, 69
Work Performance 123